NON SANZ DROICT.

THE
First part of the Con=
tention betwixt the two famous Houses of Yorke
and Lancaster, with the death of the good
Duke Humphrey:

And the banishment and death of the Duke of
Suffolke, and the Tragicall end of the proud Cardinall
of *VVinchester*, vvith the notable Rebellion
of *Iacke Cade*:

*And the Duke of Yorkes first claime vnto the
Crowne.*

LONDON
Printed by Thomas Creed, for Thomas Millington,
and are to be sold at his shop vnder Saint Peters
Church in Cornwall.
1594.

William Shakespeare

Henry VI,
Part One

Edited by Lawrence V. Ryan

Henry VI,
Part Two

Edited by Arthur Freeman

Henry VI,
Part Three

Edited by Milton Crane

With New and Updated Critical
Essays and a Revised Bibliography

THE SIGNET CLASSICS SHAKESPEARE
General Editor: Sylvan Barnet

Ⓒ

SIGNET CLASSICS

SIGNET CLASSICS
Published by New American Library, a division of
Penguin Group (USA) Inc., 375 Hudson Street,
New York, New York 10014, USA
Penguin Group (Canada), 90 Eglinton Avenue East, Suite 700, Toronto,
Ontario M4P 2Y3, Canada (a division of Pearson Penguin Canada Inc.)
Penguin Books Ltd., 80 Strand, London WC2R 0RL, England
Penguin Ireland, 25 St. Stephen's Green, Dublin 2,
Ireland (a division of Penguin Books Ltd.)
Penguin Group (Australia), 250 Camberwell Road, Camberwell, Victoria 3124,
Australia (a division of Pearson Australia Group Pty. Ltd.)
Penguin Books India Pvt. Ltd., 11 Community Centre, Panchsheel Park,
New Delhi - 110 017, India
Penguin Books (NZ), Cnr Airborne and Rosedale Roads, Albany,
Auckland 1310, New Zealand (a division of Pearson New Zealand Ltd.)
Penguin Books (South Africa) (Pty.) Ltd., 24 Sturdee Avenue,
Rosebank, Johannesburg 2196, South Africa

Penguin Books Ltd., Registered Offices:
80 Strand, London WC2R 0RL, England

Published by Signet Classics, an imprint of New American Library,
a division of Penguin Group (USA) Inc.

First Signet Classics Printing (Second Revised Edition), July 2005
10 9 8 7 6 5 4 3 2 1

Henry VI, Part One
    Copyright © Lawrence V. Ryan, 1967, 1989
    Copyright © Sylvan Barnet, 1963, 1989, 2005
Henry VI, Part Two
    Copyright © Arthur Freeman, 1967, 1989
    Copyright © Sylvan Barnet, 1963, 1989, 2005
Henry VI, Part Three
    Copyright © Milton Crane, 1968
    Copyright © Sylvan Barnet, 1963, 1989, 2005
All rights reserved

Grateful acknowledgement is made for permission to reprint portions of "Henry VI" by Ralph Fiennes from *Players of Shakespeare 3* by Russell Jackson and Robert Smallwood copyright © Cambridge University Press, 1993. Reprinted with permission of Cambridge University Press.

SIGNET CLASSICS and logo are trademarks of Penguin Group (USA) Inc.

Library of Congress Catalog Card Number: 2004059106

Printed in the United States of America

Contents

Shakespeare: An Overview
Biographical Sketch vii / *A Note on the Anti-Stratfordians, Especially Baconians and Oxfordians* xi / The Shakespeare Canon xv / Shakespeare's English xviii / Shakespeare's Theater xxvi / *A Note on the Use of Boy Actors in Female Roles* xxxiii / Shakespeare's Dramatic Language: Costumes, Gestures and Silences; Prose and Poetry xxxvi / The Play Text as a Collaboration xliii / Editing Texts xlix / Shakespeare on the Stage liv

Introduction to *Henry VI, Part One*	3
Henry VI, Part One	21
Textual Note	133
The Sources of *Henry VI, Part One*	137
RAPHAEL HOLINSHED *From* Chronicles of England, Scotland, and Ireland	139
EDWARD HALL *From* The Union of the Two Noble and Illustre Families of Lancaster and York	158
Commentaries	
HERMANN ULRICI *From* Shakspeare's Dramatic Art	161
E.M.W. TILLYARD *From* Shakespeare's History Plays	166
J. P. BROCKBANK *From* The Frame of Disorder—*Henry VI*	180
PHYLLIS RACKIN Anti-Historians: Women's Roles in Shakespeare's Histories	191
RALPH FIENNES Playing Henry VI	203

LAWRENCE V. RYAN   *Henry VI* on Stage
and Screen   206

SYLVAN BARNET   The Stage History Since 1989   224

Introduction to *Henry VI, Part Two*   235

Henry VI, Part Two   246

Textual Note   369

The Date and the Sources of *Henry VI, Part Two*   374

EDWARD HALL   *From* The Union of the Two Noble
and Illustre Families of Lancaster and York   377

JOHN FOXE   *From* Acts and Monuments of Martyrs   396

ANTHONY MUNDAY, WILLIAM SHAKESPEARE (?),
ET AL   *From* Sir Thomas More   398

Commentaries

SAMUEL JOHNSON   *From* The Plays of William
Shakespeare   404

J. P. BROCKBANK   *From* The Frame of Disorder—
Henry VI   406

Introduction to *Henry VI, Part Three*   421

Henry VI, Part Three   433

Textual Note   553

The Sources of *Henry VI, Part Three*   556

EDWARD HALL   *From* The Union of the Two Noble
and Illustre Families of Lancaster and York   559

Commentaries

SAMUEL JOHNSON   *From* The Plays of William
Shakespeare   581

J. P. BROCKBANK   *From* The Frame of Disorder—
Henry VI   587

E.M.W. TILLYARD   *From* Shakespeare's History
Plays   598

Suggested References   610

Shakespeare: An Overview

Biographical Sketch

Between the record of his baptism in Stratford on 26 April 1564 and the record of his burial in Stratford on 25 April 1616, some forty official documents name Shakespeare, and many others name his parents, his children, and his grandchildren. Further, there are at least fifty literary references to him in the works of his contemporaries. More facts are known about William Shakespeare than about any other playwright of the period except Ben Jonson. The facts should, however, be distinguished from the legends. The latter, inevitably more engaging and better known, tell us that the Stratford boy killed a calf in high style, poached deer and rabbits, and was forced to flee to London, where he held horses outside a playhouse. These traditions are only traditions; they may be true, but no evidence supports them, and it is well to stick to the facts.

Mary Arden, the dramatist's mother, was the daughter of a substantial landowner; about 1557 she married John Shakespeare, a tanner, glove-maker, and trader in wool, grain, and other farm commodities. In 1557 John Shakespeare was a member of the council (the governing body of Stratford), in 1558 a constable of the borough, in 1561 one of the two town chamberlains, in 1565 an alderman (entitling him to the appellation of "Mr."), in 1568 high bailiff—the town's highest political office, equivalent to mayor. After 1577, for an unknown reason he drops out of local politics. What *is* known is that he had to mortgage his wife's property, and that he was involved in serious litigation.

The birthday of William Shakespeare, the third child and the eldest son of this locally prominent man, is unrecorded, but the Stratford parish register records that the infant was baptized on 26 April 1564. (It is quite possible that he was born on 23 April, but this date has probably been assigned by tradition because it is the date on which, fifty-two years later, he died, and perhaps because it is the feast day of St. George, patron saint of England.) The attendance records of the Stratford grammar school of the period are not extant, but it is reasonable to assume that the son of a prominent local official attended the free school—it had been established for the purpose of educating males precisely of his class—and received substantial training in Latin. The masters of the school from Shakespeare's seventh to fifteenth years held Oxford degrees; the Elizabethan curriculum excluded mathematics and the natural sciences but taught a good deal of Latin rhetoric, logic, and literature, including plays by Plautus, Terence, and Seneca.

On 27 November 1582 a marriage license was issued for the marriage of Shakespeare and Anne Hathaway, eight years his senior. The couple had a daughter, Susanna, in May 1583. Perhaps the marriage was necessary, but perhaps the couple had earlier engaged, in the presence of witnesses, in a formal "troth plight" which would render their children legitimate even if no further ceremony were performed. In February 1585, Anne Hathaway bore Shakespeare twins, Hamnet and Judith.

That Shakespeare was born is excellent; that he married and had children is pleasant; but that we know nothing about his departure from Stratford to London or about the beginning of his theatrical career is lamentable and must be admitted. We would gladly sacrifice details about his children's baptism for details about his earliest days in the theater. Perhaps the poaching episode is true (but it is first reported almost a century after Shakespeare's death), or perhaps he left Stratford to be a schoolmaster, as another tradition holds; perhaps he was moved (like Petruchio in *The Taming of the Shrew*) by

> Such wind as scatters young men through the world,
> To seek their fortunes farther than at home
> Where small experience grows.   (1.2.49–51)

In 1592, thanks to the cantankerousness of Robert Greene, we have our first reference, a snarling one, to Shakespeare as an actor and playwright. Greene, a graduate of St. John's College, Cambridge, had become a playwright and a pamphleteer in London, and in one of his pamphlets he warns three university-educated playwrights against an actor who has presumed to turn playwright:

> There is an upstart crow, beautified with our feathers, that with his *tiger's heart wrapped in a player's hide* supposes he is as well able to bombast out a blank verse as the best of you, and being an absolute Johannes-factotum [i.e., jack-of-all-trades] is in his own conceit the only Shake-scene in a country.

The reference to the player, as well as the allusion to Aesop's crow (who strutted in borrowed plumage, as an actor struts in fine words not his own), makes it clear that by this date Shakespeare had both acted and written. That Shakespeare is meant is indicated not only by *Shake-scene* but also by the parody of a line from one of Shakespeare's plays, *3 Henry VI*: "O, tiger's heart wrapped in a woman's hide" (1.4.137). If in 1592 Shakespeare was prominent enough to be attacked by an envious dramatist, he probably had served an apprenticeship in the theater for at least a few years.

In any case, although there are no extant references to Shakespeare between the record of the baptism of his twins in 1585 and Greene's hostile comment about "Shake-scene" in 1592, it is evident that during some of these "dark years" or "lost years" Shakespeare had acted and written. There are a number of subsequent references to him as an actor. Documents indicate that in 1598 he is a "principal comedian," in 1603 a "principal tragedian," in 1608 he is one of the "men players." (We do not have, however, any solid information about which roles he may have played; later traditions say he played Adam in *As You Like It* and the ghost in *Hamlet*, but nothing supports the assertions. Probably his role as dramatist came to supersede his role as actor.) The profession of actor was not for a gentleman, and it occasionally drew the scorn of university men like Greene who resented writing speeches for persons less educated than themselves, but it was respectable enough; players, if prosperous, were in effect members of the bourgeoisie, and there is nothing to suggest that Stratford considered William Shakespeare less than a solid citizen. When, in 1596, the Shakespeares were granted a coat of arms—i.e., the right to be considered gentlemen—the grant was made to Shakespeare's father, but probably William Shakespeare had arranged the matter on his own behalf. In subsequent transactions he is occasionally styled a gentleman.

Although in 1593 and 1594 Shakespeare published two narrative poems dedicated to the Earl of Southampton, *Venus and Adonis* and *The Rape of Lucrece*, and may well have written most or all of his sonnets in the middle nineties, Shakespeare's literary activity seems to have been almost entirely devoted to the theater. (It may be significant that the two narrative poems were written in years when the plague closed the theaters for several months.) In 1594 he was a charter member of a theatrical company called the Chamberlain's Men, which in 1603 became the royal company, the King's Men, making Shakespeare the king's playwright. Until he retired to Stratford (about 1611, apparently), he was with this remarkably stable company. From 1599 the company acted primarily at the Globe theater, in which Shakespeare held a one-tenth interest. Other Elizabethan dramatists are known to have acted, but no other is known also to have been entitled to a share of the profits.

Shakespeare's first eight published plays did not have his name on them, but this is not remarkable; the most popular play of the period, Thomas Kyd's *The Spanish Tragedy*, went through many editions without naming Kyd, and Kyd's authorship is known only because a book on the profession of acting happens to quote (and attribute to Kyd) some lines on the interest of Roman emperors in the drama. What is remarkable is that after 1598 Shakespeare's name commonly appears on printed plays—some of which are not his. Presumably his name was a drawing card, and publishers used it to attract potential buyers. Another indication of his popularity comes from Francis Meres, author of *Palladis Tamia: Wit's Treasury* (1598). In this anthology of snippets accompanied by an essay on literature, many playwrights are mentioned, but Shakespeare's name occurs more often than any other, and Shakespeare is the only play-wright whose plays are listed.

From his acting, his playwriting, and his share in a playhouse, Shakespeare seems to have made considerable money. He put it to work, making substantial investments in Stratford real estate. As early as 1597 he bought New Place, the second-largest house in Stratford. His family moved in soon afterward, and the house remained in the family until a granddaughter died in 1670. When Shakespeare made his will in 1616, less than a month before he died, he sought to leave his property intact to his descendants. Of small bequests to relatives and to friends (including three actors, Richard Burbage, John Heminges, and Henry Condell), that to his wife of the second-best bed has provoked the most comment. It has sometimes been taken as a sign of an unhappy marriage (other supposed signs are the apparently hasty marriage, his wife's seniority of eight years, and his residence in London without his family). Perhaps the second-best bed was the bed the couple had slept in, the best bed being reserved for visitors. In any case, had Shakespeare not excepted it, the bed would have gone (with the rest of his household possessions) to his daughter and her husband.

On 25 April 1616 Shakespeare was buried within the chancel of the church at Stratford. An unattractive monument to his memory, placed on a wall near the grave, says that he died on 23 April. Over the grave itself are the lines, perhaps by Shakespeare, that (more than his literary fame) have kept his bones undisturbed in the crowded burial ground where old bones were often dislodged to make way for new:

> Good friend, for Jesus' sake forbear
> To dig the dust enclosed here.
> Blessed be the man that spares these stones
> And cursed be he that moves my bones.

A Note on the Anti-Stratfordians, Especially Baconians and Oxfordians

Not until 1769—more than a hundred and fifty years after Shakespeare's death—is there any record of anyone expressing doubt about Shakespeare's authorship of the plays and poems. In 1769, however, Herbert Lawrence nominated Francis Bacon (1561–1626) in *The Life and Adventures of Common Sense*. Since then, at least two dozen other nominees have been offered, including Christopher Marlowe, Sir Walter Raleigh, Queen Elizabeth I, and Edward de Vere, 17th earl of Oxford. The impulse behind all anti-Stratfordian movements is the scarcely concealed snobbish opinion that "the man from Stratford" simply could not have written the plays because he was a country fellow without a university education and without access to high society. Anyone, the argument goes, who used so many legal terms, medical terms, nautical terms, and so forth, and who showed some familiarity with classical writing, must have attended a university, and anyone who knew so much about courtly elegance and courtly deceit must himself have moved among courtiers. The plays do indeed reveal an author whose interests were exceptionally broad, but specialists in any given field—law, medicine, arms and armor, and so on—soon find that the plays do not reveal deep knowledge in specialized matters; indeed, the playwright often gets technical details wrong.

The claim on behalf of Bacon, forgotten almost as soon as it was put forth in 1769, was independently reasserted by Joseph C. Hart in 1848. In 1856 it was reaffirmed by W. H. Smith in a book, and also by Delia Bacon in an article; in 1857 Delia Bacon published a book, arguing that Francis Bacon had directed a group of intellectuals who wrote the plays.

Francis Bacon's claim has largely faded, perhaps because it was advanced with such evident craziness by Ignatius Donnelly, who in *The Great Cryptogram* (1888) claimed to break a code in the plays that proved Bacon had written not only the plays attributed to Shakespeare but also other Renaissance works, for instance the plays of Christopher Marlowe and the essays of Montaigne.

Consider the last two lines of the Epilogue in *The Tempest*:

As you from crimes would pardoned be,
Let your indulgence set me free.

What was Shakespeare—sorry, Francis Bacon, Baron Verulam—*really* saying in these two lines? According to Baconians, the lines are an anagram reading, "Tempest of Francis Bacon, Lord Verulam; do ye ne'er divulge me, ye words." Ingenious, and it is a pity that in the quotation the letter *a* appears only twice in the cryptogram, whereas in the deciphered message it appears three times. Oh, no problem; just alter "Verulam" to "Verul'm" and it works out very nicely.

Most people understand that with sufficient ingenuity one can torture any text and find in it what one wishes. For instance: Did Shakespeare have a hand in the King James Version of the Bible? It was nearing completion in 1610, when Shakespeare was forty-six years old. If you look at the 46th Psalm and count forward for forty-six words, you will find the word *shake*. Now if you go to the end of the psalm and count backward forty-six words, you will find the word *spear*. Clear evidence, according to some, that Shakespeare slyly left his mark in the book.

Bacon's candidacy has largely been replaced in the twentieth century by the candidacy of Edward de Vere (1550–1604), 17th earl of Oxford. The basic ideas behind the Oxford theory, advanced at greatest length by Dorothy and Charlton Ogburn in *This Star of England* (1952, rev. 1955), a book of 1297 pages, and by Charlton Ogburn in *The Mysterious William Shakespeare* (1984), a book of 892 pages, are these: (1) The man from Stratford could not possibly have had the mental equipment and the experience to have written the plays—only a courtier could have written them; (2) Oxford had the requisite background (social position, education, years at Queen Elizabeth's court); (3) Oxford did not wish his authorship to be known for two basic reasons: writing for the public theater was a vulgar pursuit, and the plays show so much courtly and royal disreputable behavior that they would have compromised Oxford's position at court. Oxfordians offer countless details to support the claim. For example, Hamlet's phrase "that ever I was born to set it right" (1.5.89) barely conceals "E. Ver, I was born to set it right," an unambiguous announcement of de Vere's authorship, according to *This Star of England* (p. 654). A second example: Consider Ben

Jonson's poem entitled "To the Memory of My Beloved Master William Shakespeare," prefixed to the first collected edition of Shakespeare's plays in 1623. According to Oxfordians, when Jonson in this poem speaks of the author of the plays as the "swan of Avon," he is alluding not to William Shakespeare, who was born and died in Stratford-on-Avon and who throughout his adult life owned property there; rather, he is alluding to Oxford, who, the Ogburns say, used "William Shakespeare" as his pen name, and whose manor at Bilton was on the Avon River. Oxfordians do not offer any evidence that Oxford took a pen name, and they do not care that Oxford had sold the manor in 1581, forty-two years before Jonson wrote his poem. Surely a reference to the Shakespeare who was born in Stratford, who had returned to Stratford, and who had died there only seven years before Jonson wrote the poem is more plausible. And exactly why Jonson, who elsewhere also spoke of Shakespeare as a playwright, and why Heminges and Condell, who had acted with Shakespeare for about twenty years, should speak of Shakespeare as the author in their dedication in the 1623 volume of collected plays is never adequately explained by Oxfordians. Either Jonson, Heminges and Condell, and numerous others were in on the conspiracy, or they were all duped—equally unlikely alternatives. Another difficulty in the Oxford theory is that Oxford died in 1604, and some of the plays are clearly indebted to works and events later than 1604. Among the Oxfordian responses are: At his death Oxford left some plays, and in later years these were touched up by hacks, who added the material that points to later dates. *The Tempest*, almost universally regarded as one of Shakespeare's greatest plays and pretty clearly dated to 1611, does indeed date from a period after the death of Oxford, but it is a crude piece of work that should not be included in the canon of works by Oxford.

The anti-Stratfordians, in addition to assuming that the author must have been a man of rank and a university man, usually assume two conspiracies: (1) a conspiracy in Elizabethan and Jacobean times, in which a surprisingly large number of persons connected with the theater knew that the actor Shakespeare did not write the plays attributed to him but for some reason or other pretended that he did; (2) a conspiracy of today's Stratfordians, the professors who teach Shakespeare in the colleges and universities, who are said to have a vested interest in preserving Shakespeare as the author of the plays they teach. In fact, (1) it is inconceivable that the secret of Shakespeare's nonauthorship could have been preserved by all of the people who supposedly were in on the conspiracy, and (2) academic fame awaits any scholar today who can disprove Shakespeare's authorship.

The Stratfordian case is convincing not only because hundreds or even thousands of anti-Stratford arguments—of the sort that say "ever I was born" has the secret double meaning "E. Ver, I was born"—add up to nothing at all but also because irrefutable evidence connects the man from Stratford with the London theater and with the authorship of particular plays. The anti-Stratfordians do not seem to understand that it is not enough to dismiss the Stratford case by saying that a fellow from the provinces simply couldn't have written the plays. Nor do they understand that it is not enough to dismiss all of the evidence connecting Shakespeare with the plays by asserting that it is perjured.

The Shakespeare Canon

We return to William Shakespeare. Thirty-seven plays as well as some nondramatic poems are generally held to constitute the Shakespeare canon, the body of authentic works. The exact dates of composition of most of the works are highly uncertain, but evidence of a starting point and/or of a final limiting point often provides a framework for informed guessing. For example, *Richard II* cannot be earlier than 1595, the publication date of some material to which it is indebted; *The Merchant of Venice* cannot be later than 1598, the year Francis Meres mentioned it. Sometimes arguments for a date hang on an alleged topical allusion, such as the lines about the unseasonable weather in *A Midsummer Night's Dream*, 2.1.81–117, but such an allusion, if indeed it is an allusion to an event in the real world, can be variously interpreted, and in any case there is always the possibility that a topical allusion was inserted years later, to bring the play up to date. (The issue of alterations in a text between the time that Shakespeare drafted it and the time that it was printed—alterations due to censorship or playhouse practice or Shakespeare's own second thoughts—will be discussed in "The Play Text as a Collaboration" later in this overview.) Dates are often attributed on the basis of style, and although conjectures about style usually rest on other conjectures (such as Shakespeare's development as a playwright, or the appropriateness of lines to character), sooner or later one must rely on one's literary sense. There is no documentary proof, for example, that *Othello* is not as early as *Romeo and Juliet*, but one feels that *Othello* is a later, more mature work, and because the first record of its performance is 1604, one is glad enough to set its composition at that date and not push it back into Shakespeare's early years. (*Romeo and Juliet* was first published in 1597, but evidence suggests that it was written a little earlier.) The following chronology, then, is indebted not only to facts but also to informed guesswork and sensitivity. The dates, necessarily imprecise for some works, indicate something like a scholarly consensus concerning the time of original composition. Some plays show evidence of later revision.

Plays. The first collected edition of Shakespeare, published in 1623, included thirty-six plays. These are all accepted as Shakespeare's, though for one of them, *Henry VIII*, he is thought to have had a collaborator. A thirty-seventh play, *Pericles*, published in 1609 and attributed to Shakespeare on the title page, is also widely accepted as being partly by Shakespeare even though it is not included in the 1623 volume. Still another play not in the 1623 volume, *The Two Noble Kinsmen*, was first published in 1634, with a title page attributing it to John Fletcher and Shakespeare. Probably most students of the subject now believe that Shakespeare did indeed have a hand in it. Of the remaining plays attributed at one time or another to Shakespeare, only one, *Edward III*, anonymously published in 1596, is now regarded by some scholars as a serious candidate. The prevailing opinion, however, is that this rather simple-minded play is not Shakespeare's; at most he may have revised some passages, chiefly scenes with the Countess of

Salisbury. We include *The Two Noble Kinsmen* but do not include *Edward III* in the following list.

1588–94	*The Comedy of Errors*
1588–94	*Love's Labor's Lost*
1589–91	*2 Henry VI*
1590–91	*3 Henry VI*
1589–92	*1 Henry VI*
1592–93	*Richard III*
1589–94	*Titus Andronicus*
1593–94	*The Taming of the Shrew*
1592–94	*The Two Gentlemen of Verona*
1594–96	*Romeo and Juliet*
1595	*Richard II*
1595–96	*A Midsummer Night's Dream*
1596–97	*King John*
1594–96	*The Merchant of Venice*
1596–97	*1 Henry IV*
1597	*The Merry Wives of Windsor*
1597–98	*2 Henry IV*
1598–99	*Much Ado About Nothing*
1598–99	*Henry V*
1599	*Julius Caesar*
1599–1600	*As You Like It*
1599–1600	*Twelfth Night*
1600–1601	*Hamlet*
1601–1602	*Troilus and Cressida*
1602–1604	*All's Well That Ends Well*
1603–1604	*Othello*
1604	*Measure for Measure*
1605–1606	*King Lear*
1605–1606	*Macbeth*
1606–1607	*Antony and Cleopatra*
1605–1608	*Timon of Athens*
1607–1608	*Coriolanus*
1607–1608	*Pericles*
1609–10	*Cymbeline*
1610–11	*The Winter's Tale*
1611	*The Tempest*

1612–13	*Henry VIII*
1613	*The Two Noble Kinsmen*

Poems. In 1989 Donald W. Foster published a book in which he argued that "A Funeral Elegy for Master William Peter," published in 1612, ascribed only to the initials W.S., *may* be by Shakespeare. Foster later published an article in a scholarly journal, *PMLA* 111 (1996), in which he asserted the claim more positively. The evidence begins with the initials, and includes the fact that the publisher and the printer of the elegy had published Shakespeare's *Sonnets* in 1609. But such facts add up to rather little, especially because no one has found any connection between Shakespeare and William Peter (an Oxford graduate about whom little is known, who was murdered at the age of twenty-nine). The argument is based chiefly on statistical examinations of word patterns, which are said to correlate with Shakespeare's known work. Despite such correlations, however, many readers feel that the poem does not sound like Shakespeare. True, Shakespeare has a great range of styles, but his work is consistently imaginative and interesting. Many readers find neither of these qualities in "A Funeral Elegy." The poem is now attributed to John Ford.

1592–93	*Venus and Adonis*
1593–94	*The Rape of Lucrece*
1593–1600	*Sonnets*
1600–1601	*The Phoenix and the Turtle*

Shakespeare's English

1. Spelling and Pronunciation. From the philologist's point of view, Shakespeare's English is modern English. It requires footnotes, but the inexperienced reader can comprehend substantial passages with very little help, whereas for the same reader Chaucer's Middle English is a foreign language. By the beginning of the fifteenth century the chief grammatical changes in English had taken place, and the final unaccented -*e* of Middle English had been lost (though it survives even today in spelling, as in *name*); during the fifteenth century the dialect of London, the commercial and political center, gradually displaced the provincial dialects, at least in writing; by the end of the century, printing had helped to regularize and stabilize the language, especially spelling. Elizabethan spelling may seem erratic to us (there were dozens of spellings of *Shakespeare*, and a simple word like *been* was also spelled *beene* and *bin*), but it had much in common with our spelling. Elizabethan spelling was conservative in that for the most part it reflected an older pronunciation (Middle English) rather than the sound of the language as it was then spoken, just as our spelling continues to reflect medieval pronunciation—most obviously in the now silent but formerly pronounced letters in a word such as *knight*. Elizabethan pronunciation, though not identical with ours, was much closer to ours than to that of the Middle Ages. Incidentally, though no one can be certain about what Elizabethan English sounded like, specialists tend to believe it was rather like the speech of a modern stage Irishman (*time* apparently was pronounced *toime*, *old* pronounced *awld*, *day* pronounced *die*, and *join* pronounced *jine*) and not at all like the Oxford speech that most of us think it was.

An awareness of the difference between our pronunciation and Shakespeare's is crucial in three areas—in accent, or number of syllables (many metrically regular lines may look irregular to us); in rhymes (which may not look like rhymes); and in puns (which may not look like puns). Examples will be useful. Some words that were at least on occasion stressed differently from today are *aspèct*, *còmplete*, *fòrlorn*, *revènue*, and *sepùlcher*. Words that sometimes had an additional syllable are *emp[e]ress*, *Hen[e]ry*, *mon[e]th*, and *villain* (three syllables, *vil-lay-in*). An additional syllable is often found in possessives, like *moon's* (pronounced *moones*), and in words ending in *-tion* or *-sion*. Words that had one less syllable than they now have are *needle* (pronounced *neel*) and *violet* (pronounced *vilet*). Among rhymes now lost are *one* with *loan*, *love* with *prove*, *beast* with *jest*, *eat* with *great*. (In reading, trust your sense of metrics and your ear, more than your eye.) An example of a pun that has become obliterated by a change in pronunciation is Falstaff's reply to Prince Hal's "Come, tell us your reason" in *1 Henry IV*: "Give you a reason on compulsion? If reasons were as plentiful as blackberries, I would give no man a reason upon compulsion, I" (2.4.237–40). The *ea* in *reason* was pronounced rather like a long *a,* like the *ai* in *raisin,* hence the comparison with blackberries.

Puns are not merely attempts to be funny; like metaphors they often involve bringing into a meaningful relationship areas of experience normally seen as remote. In *2 Henry IV,* when Feeble is conscripted, he stoically says, "I care not. A man can die but once. We owe God a death" (3.2.242–43), punning on *debt,* which was the way *death* was pronounced. Here an enormously significant fact of life is put into simple commercial imagery, suggesting its commonplace quality. Shakespeare used the same pun earlier in *1 Henry IV,* when Prince Hal says to Falstaff, "Why, thou owest God a death," and Falstaff replies, " 'Tis not due yet: I would be loath to pay him before his day. What need I be so forward with him that calls not on me?" (5.1.126–29).

Sometimes the puns reveal a delightful playfulness; sometimes they reveal aggressiveness, as when, replying to Claudius's "But now, my cousin Hamlet, and my son," Hamlet says, "A little more than kin, and less than kind!" (1.2.64–65). These are Hamlet's first words in the play, and we already hear him warring verbally against Claudius. Hamlet's "less than kind" probably means (1) Hamlet is not of Claudius's family or nature, *kind* having the sense it still has in our word *mankind*; (2) Hamlet is not kindly (affectionately) disposed toward Claudius; (3) Claudius is not naturally (but rather unnaturally, in a legal sense incestuously) Hamlet's father. The puns evidently were not put in as sops to the groundlings; they are an important way of communicating a complex meaning.

2. Vocabulary. A conspicuous difficulty in reading Shakespeare is rooted in the fact that some of his words are no longer in common use—for example, words concerned with armor, astrology, clothing, coinage, hawking, horsemanship, law, medicine, sailing, and war. Shakespeare had a large vocabulary—something near thirty thousand words— but it was not so much a vocabulary of big words as a vocabulary drawn from a wide range of life, and it is partly his ability to call upon a great body of concrete language that gives his plays the sense of being in close contact with life. When the right word did not already exist, he made it up. Among words thought to be his coinages are *accommodation, all-knowing, amazement, bare-faced, countless, dexterously, dislocate, dwindle, fancy-free, frugal, indistinguishable, lackluster, laughable, overawe, premeditated, sea change, star-crossed*. Among those that have not survived are the verb *convive,* meaning to feast together, and *smilet,* a little smile.

Less overtly troublesome than the technical words but more treacherous are the words that seem readily intelligible to us but whose Elizabethan meanings differ from their modern ones. When Horatio describes the Ghost as an "erring spirit," he is saying not that the ghost has sinned or made an error but that it is wandering. Here is a short list of some of the most common words in Shakespeare's plays that often (but not always) have a meaning other than their most usual modern meaning:

'a	he
abuse	deceive
accident	occurrence
advertise	inform
an, and	if
annoy	harm
appeal	accuse
artificial	skillful
brave	fine, splendid
censure	opinion
cheer	(1) face (2) frame of mind
chorus	a single person who comments on the events
closet	small private room
competitor	partner
conceit	idea, imagination
cousin	kinsman
cunning	skillful
disaster	evil astrological influence
doom	judgment
entertain	receive into service

envy	malice
event	outcome
excrement	outgrowth (of hair)
fact	evil deed
fancy	(1) love (2) imagination
fell	cruel
fellow	(1) companion (2) low person (often an insulting term if addressed to someone of approximately equal rank)
fond	foolish
free	(1) innocent (2) generous
glass	mirror
hap, haply	chance, by chance
head	army
humor	(1) mood (2) bodily fluid thought to control one's psychology
imp	child
intelligence	news
kind	natural, acting according to nature
let	hinder
lewd	base
mere(ly)	utter(ly)
modern	commonplace
natural	a fool, an idiot
naughty	(1) wicked (2) worthless
next	nearest
nice	(1) trivial (2) fussy
noise	music
policy	(1) prudence (2) stratagem
presently	immediately
prevent	anticipate
proper	handsome
prove	test
quick	alive
sad	serious
saw	proverb
secure	without care, incautious
silly	innocent

sensible	capable of being perceived by the senses
shrewd	sharp
so	provided that
starve	die
still	always
success	that which follows
tall	brave
tell	count
tonight	last night
wanton	playful, careless
watch	keep awake
will	lust
wink	close both eyes
wit	mind, intelligence

All glosses, of course, are mere approximations; sometimes one of Shakespeare's words may hover between an older meaning and a modern one, and as we have seen, his words often have multiple meanings.

3. Grammar. A few matters of grammar may be surveyed, though it should be noted at the outset that Shakespeare sometimes made up his own grammar. As E. A. Abbott says in *A Shakespearian Grammar,* "Almost any part of speech can be used as any other part of speech": a noun as a verb ("he childed as I fathered"); a verb as a noun ("She hath made compare"); or an adverb as an adjective ("a seldom pleasure"). There are hundreds, perhaps thousands, of such instances in the plays, many of which at first glance would not seem at all irregular and would trouble only a pedant. Here are a few broad matters.

Nouns: The Elizabethans thought the *-s* genitive ending for nouns (as in *man's*) derived from *his*; thus the line " 'gainst the count his galleys I did some service," for "the count's galleys."

Adjectives: By Shakespeare's time adjectives had lost the endings that once indicated gender, number, and case. About the only difference between Shakespeare's adjectives and ours is the use of the now redundant *more* or *most* with the comparative ("some more fitter place") or superlative

("This was the most unkindest cut of all"). Like double comparatives and double superlatives, double negatives were acceptable; Mercutio "will not budge for no man's pleasure."

Pronouns: The greatest change was in pronouns. In Middle English *thou, thy,* and *thee* were used among familiars and in speaking to children and inferiors; *ye, your,* and *you* were used in speaking to superiors (servants to masters, nobles to the king) or to equals with whom the speaker was not familiar. Increasingly the "polite" forms were used in all direct address, regardless of rank, and the accusative *you* displaced the nominative *ye.* Shakespeare sometimes uses *ye* instead of *you,* but even in Shakespeare's day *ye* was archaic, and it occurs mostly in rhetorical appeals.

Thou, thy, and *thee* were not completely displaced, however, and Shakespeare occasionally makes significant use of them, sometimes to connote familiarity or intimacy and sometimes to connote contempt. In *Twelfth Night* Sir Toby advises Sir Andrew to insult Cesario by addressing him as *thou:* "If thou thou'st him some thrice, it shall not be amiss" (3.2.46–47). In *Othello* when Brabantio is addressing an unidentified voice in the dark he says, "What are you?" (1.1.91), but when the voice identifies itself as the foolish suitor Roderigo, Brabantio uses the contemptuous form, saying, "I have charged thee not to haunt about my doors" (93). He uses this form for a while, but later in the scene, when he comes to regard Roderigo as an ally, he shifts back to the polite *you,* beginning in line 163, "What said she to you?" and on to the end of the scene. For reasons not yet satisfactorily explained, Elizabethans used *thou* in addresses to God—"O God, thy arm was here," the king says in *Henry V* (4.8.108)—and to supernatural characters such as ghosts and witches. A subtle variation occurs in *Hamlet.* When Hamlet first talks with the Ghost in 1.5, he uses *thou,* but when he sees the Ghost in his mother's room, in 3.4, he uses *you,* presumably because he is now convinced that the Ghost is not a counterfeit but is his father.

Perhaps the most unusual use of pronouns, from our point of view, is the neuter singular. In place of our *its, his* was often used, as in "How far that little candle throws *his* beams." But the use of a masculine pronoun for a neuter noun came to seem unnatural, and so *it* was used for the possessive as well as the nominative: "The hedge-sparrow fed the cuckoo so long / That it had it head bit off by it young." In the late sixteenth century the possessive form *its* developed, apparently by analogy with the *-s* ending used to indicate a genitive noun, as in *book*'s, but *its* was not yet common usage in Shakespeare's day. He seems to have used *its* only ten times, mostly in his later plays. Other usages, such as "you have seen Cassio and she together" or the substitution of *who* for *whom,* cause little problem even when noticed.

Verbs, Adverbs, and Prepositions: Verbs cause almost no difficulty: The third person singular present form commonly ends in *-s,* as in modern English (e.g., "He blesses"), but sometimes in *-eth* (Portia explains to Shylock that mercy "blesseth him that gives and him that takes"). Broadly speaking, the *-eth* ending was old-fashioned or dignified or "literary" rather than colloquial, except for the words *doth, hath,* and *saith.* The *-eth* ending (regularly used in the King James Bible, 1611) is very rare in Shakespeare's dramatic prose, though not surprisingly it occurs twice in the rather formal prose summary of the narrative poem *Lucrece.* Sometimes a plural subject, especially if it has collective force, takes a verb ending in *-s,* as in "My old bones aches." Some of our strong or irregular preterites (such as *broke*) have a different form in Shakespeare (*brake*); some verbs that now have a weak or regular preterite (such as *helped*) in Shakespeare have a strong or irregular preterite (*holp*). Some adverbs that today end in *-ly* were not inflected: "grievous sick," "wondrous strange." Finally, prepositions often are not the ones we expect: "We are such stuff as dreams are made on," "I have a king here to my flatterer."

Again, none of the differences (except meanings that have substantially changed or been lost) will cause much difficulty. But it must be confessed that for some elliptical passages there is no widespread agreement on meaning. Wise editors resist saying more than they know, and when they are uncertain they add a question mark to their gloss.

Shakespeare's Theater

In Shakespeare's infancy, Elizabethan actors performed wherever they could—in great halls, at court, in the courtyards of inns. These venues implied not only different audiences but also different playing conditions. The innyards must have made rather unsatisfactory theaters: on some days they were unavailable because carters bringing goods to London used them as depots; when available, they had to be rented from the innkeeper. In 1567, presumably to avoid such difficulties, and also to avoid regulation by the Common Council of London, which was not well disposed toward theatricals, one John Brayne, brother-in-law of the carpenter turned actor James Burbage, built the Red Lion in an eastern suburb of London. We know nothing about its shape or its capacity; we can say only that it may have been the first building in Europe constructed for the purpose of giving plays since the end of antiquity, a thousand years earlier. Even after the building of the Red Lion theatrical activity continued in London in makeshift circumstances, in marketplaces and inns, and always uneasily. In 1574 the Common Council required that plays and playing places in London be licensed because

> sundry great disorders and inconveniences have been found to ensue to this city by the inordinate haunting of great multitudes of people, specially youth, to plays, interludes, and shows, namely occasion of frays and quarrels, evil practices of incontinency in great inns having chambers and secret places adjoining to their open stages and galleries.

The Common Council ordered that innkeepers who wished licenses to hold performance put up a bond and make contributions to the poor.

The requirement that plays and innyard theaters be licensed, along with the other drawbacks of playing at inns and presumably along with the success of the Red Lion, led James Burbage to rent a plot of land northeast of the city walls, on property outside the jurisdiction of the city. Here he built England's second playhouse, called simply the Theatre. About all that is known of its construction is that it was wood. It soon had imitators, the most famous being the Globe (1599), essentially an amphitheater built across the Thames (again outside the city's jurisdiction), constructed with timbers of the Theatre, which had been dismantled when Burbage's lease ran out.

Admission to the theater was one penny, which allowed spectators to stand at the sides and front of the stage that jutted into the yard. An additional penny bought a seat in a covered part of the theater, and a third penny bought a more comfortable seat and a better location. It is notoriously difficult to translate prices into today's money, since some things that are inexpensive today would have been expensive in the past and vice versa—a pipeful of tobacco (imported, of course) cost a lot of money, about three pennies, and an orange (also imported) cost two or three times what a chicken cost—but perhaps we can get some idea of the low cost of the penny admission when we realize that a penny could also buy a pot of ale. An unskilled laborer made about five or sixpence a day, an artisan about twelve pence a day, and the hired actors (as opposed to the sharers in the company, such as Shakespeare) made about ten pence a performance. A printed play cost five or sixpence. Of course a visit to the theater (like a visit to a baseball game today) usually cost more than the admission since the spectator probably would also buy food and drink. Still, the low entrance fee meant that the theater was available to all except the very poorest people, rather as movies and most athletic events are today. Evidence indicates that the audience ranged from apprentices who somehow managed to scrape together the minimum entrance fee and to escape from their masters for a few hours, to prosperous members of the middle class and aristocrats who paid the additional fee for admission to the galleries. The exact proportion of men to women cannot be determined, but women of all classes certainly were present. Theaters were open every afternoon but Sundays for much of the year, except in times of plague, when they were closed because of fear of infection. By the way, no evidence suggests the presence of toilet facilities. Presumably the patrons relieved themselves by making a quick trip to the fields surrounding the playhouses.

There are four important sources of information about the

structure of Elizabethan public playhouses—drawings, a contract, recent excavations, and stage directions in the plays. Of drawings, only the so-called de Witt drawing (c. 1596) of the Swan—really his friend Aernout van Buchell's copy of Johannes de Witt's drawing—is of much significance. The drawing, the only extant representation of the interior of an Elizabethan theater, shows an amphitheater of three tiers, with a stage jutting from a wall into the yard or

Johannes de Witt, a Continental visitor to London, made a drawing of the Swan theater in about the year 1596. The original drawing is lost; this is Aernout van Buchell's copy of it.

center of the building. The tiers are roofed, and part of the stage is covered by a roof that projects from the rear and is supported at its front on two posts, but the groundlings, who paid a penny to stand in front of the stage or at its sides, were exposed to the sky. (Performances in such a playhouse were held only in the daytime; artificial illumination was not used.) At the rear of the stage are two massive doors; above the stage is a gallery.

The second major source of information, the contract for the Fortune (built in 1600), specifies that although the Globe (built in 1599) is to be the model, the Fortune is to be square, eighty feet outside and fifty-five inside. The stage is to be forty-three feet broad, and is to extend into the middle of the yard, i.e., it is twenty-seven and a half feet deep.

The third source of information, the 1989 excavations of the Rose (built in 1587), indicate that the Rose was fourteen-sided, about seventy-two feet in diameter with an inner yard almost fifty feet in diameter. The stage at the Rose was about sixteen feet deep, thirty-seven feet wide at the rear, and twenty-seven feet wide downstage. The relatively small dimensions and the tapering stage, in contrast to the rectangular stage in the Swan drawing, surprised theater historians and have made them more cautious in generalizing about the Elizabethan theater. Excavations at the Globe have not yielded much information, though some historians believe that the fragmentary evidence suggests a larger theater, perhaps one hundred feet in diameter.

From the fourth chief source, stage directions in the plays, one learns that entrance to the stage was by the doors at the rear (*"Enter one citizen at one door, and another at the other"*). A curtain hanging across the doorway—or a curtain hanging between the two doorways—could provide a place where a character could conceal himself, as Polonius does, when he wishes to overhear the conversation between Hamlet and Gertrude. Similarly, withdrawing a curtain from the doorway could "discover" (reveal) a character or two. Such discovery scenes are very rare in Elizabethan drama, but a good example occurs in *The Tempest* (5.1.171), where a stage direction tells us, *"Here Prospero discovers Ferdinand and Miranda playing at chess."* There was also some sort of playing space "aloft" or "above" to represent, for instance, the top of a city's walls or a room above the street. Doubtless each theater had its own peculiarities, but perhaps we can talk about a "typical" Elizabethan theater if we realize that no theater need exactly fit the description, just as no mother is the average mother with 2.7 children.

This hypothetical theater is wooden, round, or polygonal (in *Henry V* Shakespeare calls it a "wooden *O*"), capable of holding some eight hundred spectators who stood in the yard around the projecting elevated stage—these spectators were the "groundlings"—and some fifteen hundred additional spectators who sat in the three roofed galleries. The stage, protected by a "shadow" or "heavens" or roof, is entered from two doors; behind the doors is the "tiring house" (attiring house, i.e., dressing room), and above the stage is some sort of gallery that may sometimes hold spectators but can be used (for example) as the bedroom from which Romeo—according to a stage direction in one text—"goeth down." Some evidence suggests that a throne can be lowered onto the platform stage, perhaps from the "shadow"; certainly characters can descend from the stage through a trap or traps into the cellar or "hell." Sometimes this space beneath the stage accommodates a sound-effects man or musician (in *Antony and Cleopatra "music of the hautboys* [oboes] *is under the stage"*) or an actor (in *Hamlet* the *"Ghost cries under the stage"*). Most characters simply walk on and off through the doors, but because there is no curtain in front of the platform, corpses will have to be carried off (Hamlet obligingly clears the stage of Polonius's corpse, when he says, "I'll lug the guts into the neighbor room"). Other characters may have fallen at the rear, where a curtain on a doorway could be drawn to conceal them.

Such may have been the "public theater," so called because its inexpensive admission made it available to a wide range of the populace. Another kind of theater has been called the "private theater" because its much greater admission charge (sixpence versus the penny for general admission at the public theater) limited its audience to the wealthy or the prodigal. The private theater was basically a large room, entirely roofed and therefore artificially illuminated, with a stage at one end. The theaters thus were distinct in two ways: One was essentially an amphitheater that catered to the general public; the other was a hall that catered to the wealthy. In 1576 a hall theater was established in Blackfriars, a Dominican priory in London that had been suppressed in 1538 and confiscated by the Crown and thus was not under the city's jurisdiction. All the actors in this Blackfriars theater were boys about eight to thirteen years old (in the public theaters similar boys played female parts; a boy Lady Macbeth played to a man Macbeth). Near the end of this section on Shakespeare's theater we will talk at some length about possible implications in this convention of using boys to play female roles, but for the moment we should say that it doubtless accounts for the relative lack of female roles in Elizabethan drama. Thus, in *A Midsummer Night's Dream*, out of twenty-one named roles, only four are female; in *Hamlet*, out of twenty-four, only two (Gertrude and Ophelia) are female. Many of Shakespeare's characters have fathers but no mothers—for instance, King Lear's daughters. We need not bring in Freud to explain the disparity; a dramatic company had only a few boys in it.

To return to the private theaters, in some of which all of the performers were children—the "eyrie of . . . little eyases" (nest of unfledged hawks—2.2.347–48) which Rosencrantz mentions when he and Guildenstern talk with Hamlet. The theater in Blackfriars had a precarious existence, and ceased operations in 1584. In 1596 James Burbage, who had already made theatrical history by building the Theatre, began to construct a second Blackfriars theater. He died in 1597, and for several years this second Blackfriars theater was used by a troupe of boys, but in 1608 two of Burbage's sons and five other actors (including Shakespeare) became joint operators of the theater, using it in the winter when the open-air Globe was unsuitable. Perhaps such a smaller theater, roofed, artificially illuminated, and with a tradition of a wealthy audience, exerted an influence in Shakespeare's late plays.

Performances in the private theaters may well have had intermissions during which music was played, but in the public theaters the action was probably uninterrupted, flowing from scene to scene almost without a break. Actors would enter, speak, exit, and others would immediately enter and establish (if necessary) the new locale by a few properties and by words and gestures. To indicate that the scene took place at night, a player or two would carry a torch. Here are some samples of Shakespeare establishing the scene:

> This is Illyria, lady.   *(Twelfth Night,* 1.2.2)

> Well, this is the Forest of Arden.   *(As You Like It,* 2.4.14)

> This castle has a pleasant seat; the air
> Nimbly and sweetly recommends itself
> Unto our gentle senses.   *(Macbeth,* 1.6.1–3)

> The west yet glimmers with some streaks of day.
> > *(Macbeth,* 3.3.5)

Sometimes a speech will go far beyond evoking the minimal setting of place and time, and will, so to speak, evoke the social world in which the characters move. For instance, early in the first scene of *The Merchant of Venice* Salerio suggests an explanation for Antonio's melancholy. (In the following passage, *pageants* are decorated wagons, floats, and *cursy* is the verb "to curtsy," or "to bow.")

> Your mind is tossing on the ocean,
> There where your argosies with portly sail—
> Like signiors and rich burghers on the flood,
> Or as it were the pageants of the sea—
> Do overpeer the petty traffickers
> That cursy to them, do them reverence,
> As they fly by them with their woven wings.   (1.1.8–14)

Late in the nineteenth century, when Henry Irving produced the play with elaborate illusionistic sets, the first scene showed a ship moored in the harbor, with fruit vendors and dock laborers, in an effort to evoke the bustling and exotic life of Venice. But Shakespeare's words give us this exotic, rich world of commerce in his highly descriptive language when Salerio speaks of "argosies with portly sail" that fly with "woven wings"; equally important, through Salerio Shakespeare conveys a sense of the orderly, hierarchical society in which the lesser ships, "the petty traffickers," curtsy and thereby "do . . . reverence" to their superiors, the merchant prince's ships, which are "Like signiors and rich burghers."

On the other hand, it is a mistake to think that except for verbal pictures the Elizabethan stage was bare. Although Shakespeare's Chorus in *Henry V* calls the stage an "unworthy scaffold" (Prologue 1.10) and urges the spectators to "eke out our performance with your mind" (Prologue 3.35), there was considerable spectacle. The last act of *Macbeth,* for instance, has five stage directions calling for *"drum and colors,"* and another sort of appeal to the eye is indicated by the stage direction *"Enter Macduff, with Macbeth's head."* Some scenery and properties may have been substantial; doubtless a throne was used, but the pillars supporting the roof would have served for the trees on which Orlando pins his poems in *As You Like It.*

Having talked about the public theater—"this wooden *O*"—at some length, we should mention again that Shakespeare's plays were performed also in other locales. Alvin Kernan, in *Shakespeare, the King's Playwright: Theater in the Stuart Court 1603–1613* (1995), points out that "several of [Shakespeare's] plays contain brief theatrical performances, set always in a court or some noble house. When Shakespeare portrayed a theater, he did not, except for the choruses in *Henry V*, imagine a public theater" (p. 195). (Examples include episodes in *The Taming of the Shrew*, *A Midsummer Night's Dream*, *Hamlet*, and *The Tempest*.)

A Note on the Use of Boy Actors in Female Roles

Until fairly recently, scholars were content to mention that the convention existed; they sometimes also mentioned that it continued the medieval practice of using males in female roles, and that other theaters, notably in ancient Greece and in China and Japan, also used males in female roles. (In classical Noh drama in Japan, males still play the female roles.) Prudery may have been at the root of the academic failure to talk much about the use of boy actors, or maybe there really is not much more to say than that it was a convention of a male-centered culture (Stephen Greenblatt's view, in *Shakespearean Negotiations* [1988]). Further, the very nature of a convention is that it is not thought about: Hamlet is a Dane and Julius Caesar is a Roman, but in Shakespeare's plays they speak English, and we in the audience never give this odd fact a thought. Similarly, a character may speak in the presence of others and we understand, again without thinking about it, that he or she is not heard by the figures on the stage (the aside); a character alone on the stage may speak (the soliloquy), and we do not take the character to be unhinged; in a realistic (box) set, the fourth wall, which allows us to see what is going on, is miraculously missing. The no-nonsense view, then, is that the boy actor was an accepted convention, accepted unthinkingly—just as today we know that Kenneth Branagh is not Hamlet, Al Pacino is not Richard III, and Denzel Washington is not the Prince of Aragon. In this view, the audience takes the performer for the role, and that is that; such is the argument we now make for race-free casting, in which African-Americans and Asians can play roles of persons who lived in medieval Denmark and ancient Rome. But gender perhaps is different, at least today. It is a matter of abundant academic study: The Elizabethan theater is now sometimes called a transvestite theater, and we hear much about cross-dressing.

Shakespeare himself in a very few passages calls attention to the use of boys in female roles. At the end of *As You Like It* the boy who played Rosalind addresses the audience, and says, "O men, . . . if I were a woman, I would kiss as many of you as had beards that pleased me." But this is in the Epilogue; the plot is over, and the actor is stepping out of the play and into the audience's everyday world. A second reference to the practice of boys playing female roles occurs in *Antony and Cleopatra*, when Cleopatra imagines that she and Antony will be the subject of crude plays, her role being performed by a boy:

> The quick comedians
> Extemporally will stage us, and present
> Our Alexandrian revels: Antony
> Shall be brought drunken forth, and I shall see
> Some squeaking Cleopatra boy my greatness.   (5.2.216–20)

In a few other passages, Shakespeare is more indirect. For instance, in *Twelfth Night* Viola, played of course by a boy, disguises herself as a young man and seeks service in the house of a lord. She enlists the help of a Captain, and (by way of explaining away her voice and her beardlessness) says,

> I'll serve this duke
> Thou shalt present me as an eunuch to him.   (1.2.55–56)

In *Hamlet*, when the players arrive in 2.2, Hamlet jokes with the boy who plays a female role. The boy has grown since Hamlet last saw him: "By'r Lady, your ladyship is nearer to heaven than when I saw you last by the altitude of a chopine" (a lady's thick-soled shoe). He goes on: "Pray God your voice . . . be not cracked" (434–38).

Exactly how sexual, how erotic, this material was and is, is now much disputed. Again, the use of boys may have been unnoticed, or rather not thought about—an unexamined convention—by most or all spectators most of the time, perhaps *all* of the time, except when Shakespeare calls the convention to the attention of the audience, as in the passages just quoted. Still, an occasional bit seems to invite erotic thoughts. The clearest example is the name that Rosalind takes in *As You Like It*, Ganymede—the beautiful youth whom Zeus abducted. Did boys dressed to play female roles carry homoerotic appeal for straight men (Lisa Jardine's view, in *Still Harping on Daughters* [1983]), or for gay men, or for some or all women in the audience? Further, when the boy actor played a woman who (for the purposes of the plot) disguised herself as a male, as Rosalind, Viola, and Portia do—so we get a boy playing a woman playing a man—what sort of appeal was generated, and for what sort of spectator?

Some scholars have argued that the convention empowered women by letting female characters display a freedom unavailable in Renaissance patriarchal society; the convention, it is said, undermined rigid gender distinctions. In this view, the convention (along with plots in which female characters for a while disguised themselves as young men) allowed Shakespeare to say what some modern gender critics say: Gender is a constructed role rather than a biological given, something we make, rather than a fixed binary oppostion of male and female (see Juliet Dusinberre, in *Shakespeare and the Nature of Women* [1975]). On the other hand, some scholars have maintained that the male disguise assumed by some female characters serves only to reaffirm traditional social distinctions since female characters who don male garb (notably Portia in *The Merchant of Venice* and Rosalind in *As You Like It*) return to their female garb and at least implicitly (these critics say) reaffirm the status quo. (For this last view, see Clara Claiborne Park, in an essay in *The Woman's Part*, ed. Carolyn Ruth Swift Lenz et al. [1980].) Perhaps no one answer is right for all plays; in *As You Like It* cross-dressing empowers Rosalind, but in *Twelfth Night* cross-dressing comically traps Viola.

Shakespeare's Dramatic Language: Costumes, Gestures and Silences; Prose and Poetry

Because Shakespeare was a dramatist, not merely a poet, he worked not only with language but also with costume, sound effects, gestures, and even silences. We have already discussed some kinds of spectacle in the preceding section, and now we will begin with other aspects of visual language; a theater, after all, is literally a "place for seeing." Consider the opening stage direction in *The Tempest*, the first play in the first published collection of Shakespeare's plays: *"A tempestuous noise of thunder and Lightning heard: Enter a Ship-master, and a Boteswain."*

Costumes: What did that shipmaster and that boatswain wear? Doubtless they wore something that identified them as men of the sea. Not much is known about the costumes that Elizabethan actors wore, but at least three points are clear: (1) many of the costumes were splendid versions of contemporary Elizabethan dress; (2) some attempts were made to approximate the dress of certain occupations and of antique or exotic characters such as Romans, Turks, and Jews; (3) some costumes indicated that the wearer was supernatural. Evidence for elaborate Elizabethan clothing can be found in the plays themselves and in contemporary comments about the "sumptuous" players who wore the discarded clothing of noblemen, as well as in account books that itemize such things as "a scarlet cloak with two broad gold laces, with gold buttons down the sides."

The attempts at approximation of the dress of certain occupations and nationalities also can be documented from the plays themselves, and it derives additional confirmation from a drawing of the first scene of Shakespeare's *Titus Andronicus*—the only extant Elizabethan picture of an identifiable episode in a play. (See pp. xxxviii–xxxix.) The drawing, probably done in 1594 or 1595, shows Queen Tamora pleading for mercy. She wears a somewhat medieval-looking robe and a crown; Titus wears a toga and a wreath, but two soldiers behind him wear costumes fairly close to Elizabethan dress. We do not know, however, if the drawing represents an actual stage production in the public theater, or perhaps a private production, or maybe only a reader's visualization of an episode. Further, there is some conflicting evidence: In *Julius Caesar* a reference is made to Caesar's doublet (a close-fitting jacket), which, if taken literally, suggests that even the protagonist did not wear Roman clothing; and certainly the lesser characters, who are said to wear hats, did not wear Roman garb.

It should be mentioned, too, that even ordinary clothing can be symbolic: Hamlet's "inky cloak," for example, sets him apart from the brightly dressed members of Claudius's court and symbolizes his mourning; the fresh clothes that are put on King Lear partly symbolize his return to sanity. Consider, too, the removal of disguises near the end of some plays. For instance, Rosalind in *As You Like It* and Portia and Nerissa in *The Merchant of Venice* remove their male attire, thus again becoming fully themselves.

Gestures and Silences: Gestures are an important part of a dramatist's language. King Lear kneels before his daughter Cordelia for a benediction (4.7.57–59), an act of humility that contrasts with his earlier speeches banishing her and that contrasts also with a comparable gesture, his ironic

kneeling before Regan (2.4.153–55). Northumberland's failure to kneel before King Richard II (3.3.71–72) speaks volumes. As for silences, consider a moment in *Coriolanus*: Before the protagonist yields to his mother's entreaties (5.3.182), there is this stage direction: *"Holds her by the hand, silent."* Another example of "speech in dumbness" occurs in *Macbeth*, when Macduff learns that his wife and children have been murdered. He is silent at first, as Malcolm's speech indicates: "What, man! Ne'er pull your hat upon your brows. Give sorrow words" (4.3.208–9). (For a discussion of such moments, see Philip C. McGuire's *Speechless Dialect: Shakespeare's Open Silences* [1985].)

Of course when we think of Shakespeare's work, we think primarily of his language, both the poetry and the prose.

Prose: Although two of his plays (*Richard II* and *King John*) have no prose at all, about half the others have at least one quarter of the dialogue in prose, and some have notably more: *1 Henry IV* and *2 Henry IV*, about half; *As You Like It*

and *Twelfth Night*, a little more than half; *Much Ado About Nothing*, more than three quarters; and *The Merry Wives of Windsor*, a little more than five-sixths. We should remember that despite Molière's joke about M. Jourdain, who was amazed to learn that he spoke prose, most of us do not speak prose. Rather, we normally utter repetitive, shapeless, and often ungrammatical torrents; prose is something very different—a sort of literary imitation of speech at its most coherent.

Today we may think of prose as "natural" for drama; or even if we think that poetry is appropriate for high tragedy we may still think that prose is the right medium for comedy. Greek, Roman, and early English comedies, however, were written in verse. In fact, prose was not generally considered a literary medium in England until the late fifteenth century; Chaucer tells even his bawdy stories in verse. By the end of the 1580s, however, prose had established itself on the English comic stage. In tragedy, Marlowe made some use of prose, not simply in the speeches of clownish servants but even in the speech of a tragic hero, Doctor Faustus. Still, before Shakespeare, prose normally was used in the theater only for special circumstances: (1) letters and proclamations, to set them off from the poetic dialogue; (2) mad characters, to indicate that normal thinking has become disordered; and (3) low comedy, or speeches uttered by clowns even when they are not being comic. Shakespeare made use of these conventions, but he also went far beyond them. Sometimes he begins a scene in prose and then shifts into verse as the emotion is heightened; or conversely, he may shift from verse to prose when a speaker is lowering the emotional level, as when Brutus speaks in the Forum.

Shakespeare's prose usually is not prosaic. Hamlet's prose includes not only small talk with Rosencrantz and Guildenstern but also princely reflections on "What a piece of work is a man" (2.2.312). In conversation with Ophelia, he shifts from light talk in verse to a passionate prose denunciation of women (3.1.103), though the shift to prose here is perhaps also intended to suggest the possibility of madness. (Consult Brian Vickers, *The Artistry of Shakespeare's Prose* [1968].)

Poetry: Drama in rhyme in England goes back to the Middle Ages, but by Shakespeare's day rhyme no longer dominated poetic drama; a finer medium, blank verse (strictly speaking, unrhymed lines of ten syllables, with the stress on every second syllable) had been adopted. But before looking at unrhymed poetry, a few things should be said about the chief uses of rhyme in Shakespeare's plays. (1) A couplet (a pair of rhyming lines) is sometimes used to convey emotional heightening at the end of a blank verse speech; (2) characters sometimes speak a couplet as they leave the stage, suggesting closure; (3) except in the latest plays, scenes fairly often conclude with a couplet, and sometimes, as in *Richard II*, 2.1.145–46, the entrance of a new character within a scene is preceded by a couplet, which wraps up the earlier portion of that scene; (4) speeches of two characters occasionally are linked by rhyme, most notably in *Romeo and Juliet*, 1.5.95–108, where the lovers speak a sonnet between them; elsewhere a taunting reply occasionally rhymes with the previous speaker's last line; (5) speeches with sententious or gnomic remarks are sometimes in rhyme, as in the duke's speech in *Othello* (1.3.199–206); (6) speeches of sardonic mockery are sometimes in rhyme—for example, Iago's speech on women in *Othello* (2.1.146–58)—and they sometimes conclude with an emphatic couplet, as in Bolingbroke's speech on comforting words in *Richard II* (1.3.301–2); (7) some characters are associated with rhyme, such as the fairies in *A Midsummer Night's Dream*; (8) in the early plays, especially *The Comedy of Errors* and *The Taming of the Shrew*, comic scenes that in later plays would be in prose are in jingling rhymes; (9) prologues, choruses, plays-within-the-play, inscriptions, vows, epilogues, and so on are often in rhyme, and the songs in the plays are rhymed.

Neither prose nor rhyme immediately comes to mind when we first think of Shakespeare's medium: It is blank verse, unrhymed iambic pentameter. (In a mechanically exact line there are five iambic feet. An iambic foot consists of two syllables, the second accented, as in *away*; five feet make a pentameter line. Thus, a strict line of iambic pentameter contains ten syllables, the even syllables being stressed more heavily than the odd syllables. Fortunately, Shakespeare usually varies the line somewhat.) The first speech in *A Midsummer Night's Dream*, spoken by Duke Theseus to his betrothed, is an example of blank verse:

> Now, fair Hippolyta, our nuptial hour
> Draws on apace. Four happy days bring in
> Another moon; but, O, methinks, how slow
> This old moon wanes! She lingers my desires,
> Like to a stepdame, or a dowager,
> Long withering out a young man's revenue.   (1.1.1–6)

As this passage shows, Shakespeare's blank verse is not mechanically unvarying. Though the predominant foot is the iamb (as in *apace* or *desires*), there are numerous variations. In the first line the stress can be placed on "fair," as the regular metrical pattern suggests, but it is likely that "Now" gets almost as much emphasis; probably in the second line "Draws" is more heavily emphasized than "on," giving us a trochee (a stressed syllable followed by an unstressed one); and in the fourth line each word in the phrase "This old moon wanes" is probably stressed fairly heavily, conveying by two spondees (two feet, each of two stresses) the oppressive tedium that Theseus feels.

In Shakespeare's early plays much of the blank verse is end-stopped (that is, it has a heavy pause at the end of each line), but he later developed the ability to write iambic pentameter verse paragraphs (rather than lines) that give the illusion of speech. His chief techniques are (1) enjambing, i.e., running the thought beyond the single line, as in the first three lines of the speech just quoted; (2) occasionally replacing an iamb with another foot; (3) varying the position of the chief pause (the caesura) within a line; (4) adding an occasional unstressed syllable at the end of a line, traditionally called a feminine ending; and (5) beginning or ending a speech with a half line.

Shakespeare's mature blank verse has much of the rhythmic flexibility of his prose; both the language, though richly figurative and sometimes dense, and the syntax seem natural. It is also often highly appropriate to a particular character. Consider, for instance, this speech from *Hamlet*, in which Claudius, King of Denmark ("the Dane"), speaks to Laertes:

> And now, Laertes, what's the news with you?
> You told us of some suit. What is't, Laertes?
> You cannot speak of reason to the Dane
> And lose your voice. What wouldst thou beg, Laertes,
> That shall not be my offer, not thy asking?   (1.2.42–46)

Notice the short sentences and the repetition of the name "Laertes," to whom the speech is addressed. Notice, too, the shift from the royal "us" in the second line to the more intimate "my" in the last line, and from "you" in the first three lines to the more intimate "thou" and "thy" in the last two lines. Claudius knows how to ingratiate himself with Laertes.

For a second example of the flexibility of Shakespeare's blank verse, consider a passage from *Macbeth*. Distressed by the doctor's inability to cure Lady Macbeth and by the imminent battle, Macbeth addresses some of his remarks to the doctor and others to the servant who is arming him. The entire speech, with its pauses, interruptions, and irresolution (in "Pull't off, I say," Macbeth orders the servant to remove the armor that the servant has been putting on him), catches Macbeth's disintegration. (In the first line, *physic* means "medicine," and in the fourth and fifth lines, *cast the water* means "analyze the urine.")

> Throw physic to the dogs, I'll none of it.
> Come, put mine armor on. Give me my staff.
> Seyton, send out.—Doctor, the thanes fly from me.—
> Come, sir, dispatch. If thou couldst, doctor, cast
> The water of my land, find her disease
> And purge it to a sound and pristine health,
> I would applaud thee to the very echo,
> That should applaud again.—Pull't off, I say.—
> What rhubarb, senna, or what purgative drug,
> Would scour these English hence? Hear'st thou of them?
>
> (5.3.47–56)

Blank verse, then, can be much more than unrhymed iambic pentameter, and even within a single play Shakespeare's blank verse often consists of several styles, depending on the speaker and on the speaker's emotion at the moment.

The Play Text as a Collaboration

Shakespeare's fellow dramatist Ben Jonson reported that the actors said of Shakespeare, "In his writing, whatsoever he penned, he never blotted out line," i.e., never crossed out material and revised his work while composing. None of Shakespeare's plays survives in manuscript (with the possible exception of a scene in *Sir Thomas More*), so we cannot fully evaluate the comment, but in a few instances the published work clearly shows that he revised his manuscript. Consider the following passage (shown here in facsimile) from the best early text of *Romeo and Juliet*, the Second Quarto (1599):

Ro. Would I were sleepe and peace so sweet to rest
The grey eyde morne smiles on the frowning night,
Checkring the Easterne Clouds with streaks of light,
And darknesse fleckted like a drunkard reeles,
From forth daies pathway, made by *Tytans* wheeles.
Hence will I to my ghostly Friers close cell,
His helpe to craue, and my deare hap to tell.

                                        Exit.

Enter Frier alone with a basket.   (night,
Fri. The grey-eyed morne smiles on the frowning
Checking the Easterne clowdes with streaks of light:
And fleckeld darknesse like a drunkard reeles,
From forth daies path, and *Titans* burning wheeles:
Now ere the sun aduance his burning eie,

Romeo rather elaborately tells us that the sun at dawn is
dispelling the night (morning is smiling, the eastern clouds
are checked with light, and the sun's chariot—Titan's
wheels—advances), and he will seek out his spiritual father,
the Friar. He exits and, oddly, the Friar enters and says pretty
much the same thing about the sun. Both speakers say that
"the gray-eyed morn smiles on the frowning night," but there
are small differences, perhaps having more to do with the
business of printing the book than with the author's
composition: For Romeo's "checkring," "fleckted," and
"pathway," we get the Friar's "checking," "fleckeld," and
"path." (Notice, by the way, the inconsistency in Elizabethan
spelling: Romeo's "clouds" become the Friar's "clowdes.")
  Both versions must have been in the printer's copy, and it
seems safe to assume that both were in Shakespeare's manuscript. He must have written one version—let's say he first
wrote Romeo's closing lines for this scene—and then he
decided, no, it's better to give this lyrical passage to the
Friar, as the opening of a new scene, but he neglected to
delete the first version. Editors must make a choice, and they
may feel that the reasonable thing to do is to print the text as
Shakespeare intended it. But how can we know what he
intended? Almost all modern editors delete the lines from

Romeo's speech, and retain the Friar's lines. They don't do this because they know Shakespeare's intention, however. They give the lines to the Friar because the first published version (1597) of *Romeo and Juliet* gives only the Friar's version, and this text (though in many ways inferior to the 1599 text) is thought to derive from the memory of some actors, that is, it is thought to represent a performance, not just a script. Maybe during the course of rehearsals Shakespeare—an actor as well as an author—unilaterally decided that the Friar should speak the lines; if so (remember that we don't know this to be a fact) his final intention was to give the speech to the Friar. Maybe, however, the actors talked it over and settled on the Friar, with or without Shakespeare's approval. On the other hand, despite the 1597 version, one might argue (if only weakly) on behalf of giving the lines to Romeo rather than to the Friar, thus: (1) Romeo's comment on the coming of the daylight emphasizes his separation from Juliet, and (2) the figurative language seems more appropriate to Romeo than to the Friar. Having said this, in the Signet edition we have decided in this instance to draw on the evidence provided by earlier text and to give the lines to the Friar, on the grounds that since Q1 reflects a production, in the theater (at least on one occasion) the lines were spoken by the Friar.

A playwright sold a script to a theatrical company. The script thus belonged to the company, not the author, and author and company alike must have regarded this script not as a literary work but as the basis for a play that the actors would create on the stage. We speak of Shakespeare as the author of the plays, but readers should bear in mind that the texts they read, even when derived from a single text, such as the First Folio (1623), are inevitably the collaborative work not simply of Shakespeare with his company—doubtless during rehearsals the actors would suggest alterations—but also with other forces of the age. One force was governmental censorship. In 1606 parliament passed "an Act to restrain abuses of players," prohibiting the utterance of oaths and the name of God. So where the earliest text of *Othello* gives us "By heaven" (3.3.106), the first Folio gives "Alas," presumably reflecting the compliance of stage practice with the law. Similarly, the 1623 version of *King Lear* omits the oath "Fut" (probably from "By God's foot") at 1.2.142, again presumably reflecting the line as it was spoken on the stage. Editors who seek to give the reader the play that Shakespeare initially conceived—the "authentic" play conceived by the solitary Shakespeare—probably will restore the missing oaths and references to God. Other editors, who see the play as a collaborative work, a construction made not only by Shakespeare but also by actors and compositors and even government censors, may claim that what counts is the play as it was actually performed. Such editors regard the censored text as legitimate, since it is the play that was (presumably) finally put on. A performed text, they argue, has more historical reality than a text produced by an editor who has sought to get at what Shakespeare initially wrote. In this view, the text of a play is rather like the script of a film; the script is not the film, and the play text is not the performed play. Even if we want to talk about the play that Shakespeare "intended," we will find ourselves talking about a script that he handed over to a company with the intention that it be implemented by actors. The "intended" play is the one that the actors—we might almost say "society"—would help to construct.

Further, it is now widely held that a play is also the work of readers and spectators, who do not simply receive meaning, but who create it when they respond to the play. This idea is fully in accord with contemporary poststructuralist critical thinking, notably Roland Barthes's "The Death of the Author," in *Image-Music-Text* (1977) and Michel Foucault's "What Is an Author?", in *The Foucault Reader* (1984). The gist of the idea is that an author is not an isolated genius; rather, authors are subject to the politics and other social structures of their age. A dramatist especially is a worker in a collaborative project, working most obviously with actors—parts may be written for particular actors—but working also with the audience. Consider the words of Samuel Johnson, written to be spoken by the actor David Garrick at the opening of a theater in 1747:

> The stage but echoes back the public voice;
> The drama's laws, the drama's patrons give,
> For we that live to please, must please to live.

The audience—the public taste as understood by the playwright—helps to determine what the play is. Moreover, even members of the public who are not part of the playwright's immediate audience may exert an influence through censorship. We have already glanced at governmental censorship, but there are also other kinds. Take one of Shakespeare's most beloved characters, Falstaff, who appears in three of Shakespeare's plays, the two parts of *Henry IV* and *The Merry Wives of Windsor*. He appears with this name in the earliest printed version of the first of these plays, *1 Henry IV*, but we know that Shakespeare originally called him (after an historical figure) Sir John Oldcastle. Oldcastle appears in Shakespeare's source (partly reprinted in the Signet edition of *1 Henry IV*), and a trace of the name survives in Shakespeare's play, 1.2.43–44, where Prince Hal punningly addresses Falstaff as "my old lad of the castle." But for some reason—perhaps because the family of the historical Oldcastle complained—Shakespeare had to change the name. In short, the play as we have it was (at least in this detail) subject to some sort of censorship. If we think that a text should present what we take to be the author's intention, we probably will want to replace *Falstaff* with *Oldcastle*. But if we recognize that a play is a collaboration, we may welcome the change, even if it was forced on Shakespeare. Somehow *Falstaff*, with its hint of *false-staff*, i.e., inadequate prop, seems just right for this fat knight who, to our delight, entertains the young prince with untruths. We can go as far as saying that, at least so far as a play is concerned, an insistence on the author's original intention (even if we could know it) can sometimes impoverish the text.

The tiny example of Falstaff's name illustrates the point that the text we read is inevitably only a version—something in effect produced by the collaboration of the playwright with his actors, audiences, compositors, and editors—of a fluid text that Shakespeare once wrote, just as the *Hamlet* that we see on the screen starring Kenneth Branagh is not the *Hamlet* that Shakespeare saw in an open-air playhouse starring Richard Burbage. *Hamlet* itself, as we shall note in a moment, also exists in several versions. It is not surprising that there is now much talk about the *instability* of Shakespeare's texts.

Because he was not only a playwright but was also an actor and a shareholder in a theatrical company, Shakespeare probably was much involved with the translation of the play from a manuscript to a stage production. He may or may not have done some rewriting during rehearsals, and he may or may not have been happy with cuts that were made. Some plays, notably *Hamlet* and *King Lear*, are so long that it is most unlikely that the texts we read were acted in their entirety. Further, for both of these plays we have more than one early text that demands consideration. In *Hamlet*, the Second Quarto (1604) includes some two hundred lines not found in the Folio (1623). Among the passages missing from the Folio are two of Hamlet's reflective speeches, the "dram of evil" speech (1.4.13–38) and "How all occasions do inform against me" (4.4.32–66). Since the Folio has more numerous and often fuller stage directions, it certainly looks as though in the Folio we get a theatrical version of the play, a text whose cuts were probably made—this is only a hunch, of course—not because Shakespeare was changing his conception of Hamlet but because the playhouse demanded a modified play. (The problem is complicated, since the Folio not only cuts some of the Quarto but adds some material. Various explanations have been offered.)

Or take an example from *King Lear*. In the First and Second Quarto (1608, 1619), the final speech of the play is given to Albany, Lear's surviving son-in-law, but in the First Folio version (1623), the speech is given to Edgar. The Quarto version is in accord with tradition—usually the highest-ranking character in a tragedy speaks the final words. Why does the Folio give the speech to Edgar? One possible answer is this: The Folio version omits some of Albany's speeches in earlier scenes, so perhaps it was decided (by Shakespeare? by the players?) not to give the final lines to so pale a character. In fact, the discrepancies are so many between the two texts, that some scholars argue we do not simply have texts showing different theatrical productions. Rather, these scholars say, Shakespeare substantially revised the play, and we really have two versions of *King Lear* (and of *Othello* also, say some)—two different plays—not simply two texts, each of which is in some ways imperfect.

In this view, the 1608 version of *Lear* may derive from Shakespeare's manuscript, and the 1623 version may derive from his later revision. The Quartos have almost three hundred lines not in the Folio, and the Folio has about a hundred lines not in the Quartos. It used to be held that all the texts were imperfect in various ways and from various causes—some passages in the Quartos were thought to have been set from a manuscript that was not entirely legible, other passages were thought to have been set by a compositor who was new to setting plays, and still other passages were thought to have been provided by an actor who misremembered some of the lines. This traditional view held that an editor must draw on the Quartos and the Folio in order to get Shakespeare's "real" play. The new argument holds (although not without considerable strain) that we have two authentic plays, Shakespeare's early version (in the Quarto) and Shakespeare's—or his theatrical company's—revised version (in the Folio). Not only theatrical demands but also Shakespeare's own artistic sense, it is argued, called for extensive revisions. Even the titles vary: Q1 is called *True Chronicle Historie of the life and death of King Lear and his three Daughters*, whereas the Folio text is called *The Tragedie of King Lear*. To combine the two texts in order to produce what the editor thinks is the play that Shakespeare intended to write is, according to this view, to produce a text that is false to the history of the play. If the new view is correct, and we do have texts of two distinct versions of *Lear* rather than two imperfect versions of one play, it supports in a textual way the poststructuralist view that we cannot possibly have an unmediated vision of (in this case) a play by Shakespeare; we can only recognize a plurality of visions.

Editing Texts

Though eighteen of his plays were published during his lifetime, Shakespeare seems never to have supervised their publication. There is nothing unusual here; when a playwright sold a play to a theatrical company he surrendered his ownership to it. Normally a company would not publish the play, because to publish it meant to allow competitors to acquire the piece. Some plays did get published: Apparently hard-up actors sometimes pieced together a play for a publisher; sometimes a company in need of money sold a play; and sometimes a company allowed publication of a play that no longer drew audiences. That Shakespeare did not concern himself with publication is not remarkable; of his contemporaries, only Ben Jonson carefully supervised the publication of his own plays.

In 1623, seven years after Shakespeare's death, John Heminges and Henry Condell (two senior members of Shakespeare's company, who had worked with him for about twenty years) collected his plays—published and unpublished—into a large volume, of a kind called a folio. (A folio is a volume consisting of large sheets that have been folded once, each sheet thus making two leaves, or four pages. The size of the page of course depends on the size of the sheet—a folio can range in height from twelve to sixteen inches, and in width from eight to eleven; the pages in the 1623 edition of Shakespeare, commonly called the First Folio, are approximately thirteen inches tall and eight inches wide.) The eighteen plays published during Shakespeare's lifetime had been issued one play per volume in small formats called quartos. (Each sheet in a quarto has been folded twice, making four leaves, or eight pages, each page being about nine inches tall and seven inches wide, roughly the size of a large paperback.)

Heminges and Condell suggest in an address "To the great variety of readers" that the republished plays are presented in better form than in the quartos:

> Before you were abused with diverse stolen and surreptitious copies, maimed and deformed by the frauds and stealths of injurious impostors that exposed them; even those, are now offered to your view cured and perfect of their limbs, and all the rest absolute in their numbers, as he [i.e., Shakespeare] conceived them.

There is a good deal of truth to this statement, but some of the quarto versions are better than others; some are in fact preferable to the Folio text.

Whoever was assigned to prepare the texts for publication in the first Folio seems to have taken the job seriously and yet not to have performed it with uniform care. The sources of the

texts seem to have been, in general, good unpublished copies
or the best published copies. The first play in the collection,
The Tempest, is divided into acts and scenes, has unusually
full stage directions and descriptions of spectacle, and concludes with a list of the characters, but the editor was not able
(or willing) to present all of the succeeding texts so fully
dressed. Later texts occasionally show signs of carelessness:
in one scene of *Much Ado About Nothing* the names of actors,
instead of characters, appear as speech prefixes, as they had in
the Quarto, which the Folio reprints; proofreading throughout
the Folio is spotty and apparently was done without reference
to the printer's copy; the pagination of *Hamlet* jumps from
156 to 257. Further, the proofreading was done while the
presses continued to print, so that each play in each volume
contains a mix of corrected and uncorrected pages.

Modern editors of Shakespeare must first select their
copy; no problem if the play exists only in the Folio, but a
considerable problem if the relationship between a Quarto
and the Folio—or an early Quarto and a later one—is
unclear. In the case of *Romeo and Juliet*, the First Quarto
(Q1), published in 1597, is vastly inferior to the Second
(Q2), published in 1599. The basis of Q1 apparently is a version put together from memory by some actors. Not surprisingly, it garbles many passages and is much shorter than Q2.
On the other hand, occasionally Q1 makes better sense than
Q2. For instance, near the end of the play, when the parents
have assembled and learned of the deaths of Romeo and
Juliet, in Q2 the Prince says (5.3.208–9),

> Come, *Montague;* for thou art early vp
> To see thy sonne and heire, now earling downe.

The last three words of this speech surely do not make sense,
and many editors turn to Q1, which instead of "now earling
downe" has "more early downe." Some modern editors take
only "early" from Q1, and print "now early down"; others
take "more early," and print "more early down." Further, Q1
(though, again, quite clearly a garbled and abbreviated text)
includes some stage directions that are not found in Q2, and
today many editors who base their text on Q2 are glad to add
these stage directions, because the directions help to give us

a sense of what the play looked like on Shakespeare's stage. Thus, in 4.3.58, after Juliet drinks the potion, Q1 gives us this stage direction, not in Q2: *"She falls upon her bed within the curtains."*

In short, an editor's decisions do not end with the choice of a single copy text. First of all, editors must reckon with Elizabethan spelling. If they are not producing a facsimile, they probably modernize the spelling, but ought they to preserve the old forms of words that apparently were pronounced quite unlike their modern forms—*lanthorn, alablaster*? If they preserve these forms are they really preserving Shakespeare's forms or perhaps those of a compositor in the printing house? What is one to do when one finds *lanthorn* and *lantern* in adjacent lines? (The editors of this series in general, but not invariably, assume that words should be spelled in their modern form, unless, for instance, a rhyme is involved.) Elizabethan punctuation, too, presents problems. For example, in the First Folio, the only text for the play, Macbeth rejects his wife's idea that he can wash the blood from his hand (2.2.60–62):

> No: this my Hand will rather
> The multitudinous Seas incarnardine,
> Making the Greene one, Red.

Obviously an editor will remove the superfluous capitals, and will probably alter the spelling to "incarnadine," but what about the comma before "Red"? If we retain the comma, Macbeth is calling the sea "the green one." If we drop the comma, Macbeth is saying that his bloody hand will make the sea ("the Green") *uniformly* red.

An editor will sometimes have to change more than spelling and punctuation. Macbeth says to his wife (1.7.46–47):

> I dare do all that may become a man,
> Who dares no more, is none.

For two centuries editors have agreed that the second line is unsatisfactory, and have emended "no" to "do": "Who dares do more is none." But when in the same play (4.2.21–22) Ross says that fearful persons

Floate vpon a wilde and violent Sea
Each way, and moue,

need we emend the passage? On the assumption that the compositor misread the manuscript, some editors emend "each way, and move" to "and move each way"; others emend "move" to "none" (i.e., "Each way and none"). Other editors, however, let the passage stand as in the original. The editors of the Signet Classic Shakespeare have restrained themselves from making abundant emendations. In their minds they hear Samuel Johnson on the dangers of emendation: "I have adopted the Roman sentiment, that it is more honorable to save a citizen than to kill an enemy." Some departures (in addition to spelling, punctuation, and lineation) from the copy text have of course been made, but the original readings are listed in a note following the play, so that readers can evaluate the changes for themselves.

Following tradition, the editors of the Signet Classic Shakespeare have prefaced each play with a list of characters, and throughout the play have regularized the names of the speakers. Thus, in our text of *Romeo and Juliet*, all speeches by Juliet's mother are prefixed "Lady Capulet," although the 1599 Quarto of the play, which provides our copy text, uses at various points seven speech tags for this one character: *Capu. Wi.* (i.e., Capulet's wife), *Ca. Wi., Wi., Wife, Old La.* (i.e., Old Lady), *La.,* and *Mo.* (i.e., Mother). Similarly, in *All's Well That Ends Well*, the character whom we regularly call "Countess" is in the Folio (the copy text) variously identified as *Mother, Countess, Old Countess, Lady,* and *Old Lady.* Admittedly there is some loss in regularizing, since the various prefixes may give us a hint of the way Shakespeare (or a scribe who copied Shakespeare's manuscript) was thinking of the character in a particular scene—for instance, as a mother, or as an old lady. But too much can be made of these differing prefixes, since the social relationships implied are *not* always relevant to the given scene.

We have also added line numbers and in many cases act and scene divisions as well as indications of locale at the beginning of scenes. The Folio divided most of the plays into acts and some into scenes. Early eighteenth-century editors increased the divisions. These divisions, which provide a convenient way of referring to passages in the plays, have been retained, but when not in the text chosen as the basis for the Signet Classic text they are enclosed within square brackets, [ ], to indicate that they are editorial additions. Similarly, though no play of Shakespeare's was equipped with indications of the locale at the heads of scene divisions, locales have here been added in square brackets for the convenience of readers, who lack the information that costumes, properties, gestures, and scenery afford to spectators. Spectators can tell at a glance they are in the throne room, but without an editorial indication the reader may be puzzled for a while. It should be mentioned, incidentally, that there are a few authentic stage directions—perhaps Shakespeare's, perhaps a prompter's—that suggest locales, such as *"Enter Brutus in his orchard,"* and *"They go up into the Senate house."* It is hoped that the bracketed additions in the Signet text will provide readers with the sort of help provided by these two authentic directions, but it is equally hoped that the reader will remember that the stage was not loaded with scenery.

Shakespeare on the Stage

Each volume in the Signet Classic Shakespeare includes a brief stage (and sometimes film) history of the play. When we read about earlier productions, we are likely to find them eccentric, obviously wrongheaded—for instance, Nahum Tate's version of *King Lear*, with a happy ending, which held the stage for about a century and a half, from the late seventeenth century until the end of the first quarter of the nineteenth. We see engravings of David Garrick, the greatest actor of the eighteenth century, in eighteenth-century garb as King Lear, and we smile, thinking how absurd the production must have been. If we are more thoughtful, we say, with the English novelist L. P. Hartley, "The past is a foreign country: they do things differently there." But if the eighteenth-century staging is a foreign country, what of the plays of the late sixteenth and seventeenth centuries? A foreign language, a foreign theater, a foreign audience.

Probably all viewers of Shakespeare's plays, beginning with Shakespeare himself, at times have been unhappy with the plays on the stage. Consider three comments about production that we find in the plays themselves, which suggest Shakespeare's concerns. The Chorus in *Henry V* complains that the heroic story cannot possibly be adequately staged:

> But pardon, gentles all,
> The flat unraisèd spirits that hath dared
> On this unworthy scaffold to bring forth
> So great an object. Can this cockpit hold
> The vasty fields of France? Or may we cram
> Within this wooden *O* the very casques
> That did affright the air at Agincourt?
> . . . .
> Piece out our imperfections with your thoughts.
>
> (Prologue 1.8–14, 23)

Second, here are a few sentences (which may or may not represent Shakespeare's own views) from Hamlet's longish lecture to the players:

> Speak the speech, I pray you, as I pronounced it to you, trippingly on the tongue. But if you mouth it, as many of our players do, I had as lief the town crier spoke my lines. . . . O, it offends me to the soul to hear a robustious periwig-pated fellow tear a passion to tatters, to very rags, to split the ears of the groundlings. . . . And let those that play your clowns speak no more than is set down for them, for there be of them that will themselves laugh, to set on some quantity of barren spectators to laugh too, though in the meantime some necessary question of the play be then to be considered. That's villainous and shows a most pitiful ambition in the fool that uses it. (3.2.1–47)

Finally, we can quote again from the passage cited earlier in this introduction, concerning the boy actors who played the female roles. Cleopatra imagines with horror a theatrical version of her activities with Antony:

> The quick comedians
> Extemporally will stage us, and present
> Our Alexandrian revels: Antony
> Shall be brought drunken forth, and I shall see

Some squeaking Cleopatra boy my greatness
I' th' posture of a whore.   (5.2.216–21)

It is impossible to know how much weight to put on such
passages—perhaps Shakespeare was just being modest
about his theater's abilities—but it is easy enough to think
that he was unhappy with some aspects of Elizabethan production. Probably no production can fully satisfy a playwright, and for that matter, few productions can fully satisfy
us; we regret this or that cut, this or that way of costuming
the play, this or that bit of business.

One's first thought may be this: Why don't they just do
"authentic" Shakespeare, "straight" Shakespeare, the play
as Shakespeare wrote it? But as we read the plays—words
written to be performed—it sometimes becomes clear that
we do not know *how* to perform them. For instance, in
Antony and Cleopatra Antony, the Roman general who has
succumbed to Cleopatra and to Egyptian ways, says, "The
nobleness of life / Is to do thus" (1.1.36–37). But what is
"thus"? Does Antony at this point embrace Cleopatra? Does
he embrace and kiss her? (There are, by the way, very few
scenes of kissing on Shakespeare's stage, possibly because
boys played the female roles.) Or does he make a sweeping
gesture, indicating the Egyptian way of life?

This is not an isolated example; the plays are filled with
lines that call for gestures, but we are not sure what the gestures should be. *Interpretation* is inevitable. Consider a passage in *Hamlet.* In 3.1, Polonius persuades his daughter,
Ophelia, to talk to Hamlet while Polonius and Claudius
eavesdrop. The two men conceal themselves, and Hamlet
encounters Ophelia. At 3.1.131 Hamlet suddenly says to her,
"Where's your father?" Why does Hamlet, apparently out of
nowhere—they have not been talking about Polonius—ask
this question? Is this an example of the "antic disposition"
(fantastic behavior) that Hamlet earlier (1.5.172) had told
Horatio and others—including us—he would display? That
is, is the question about the whereabouts of her father a
seemingly irrational one, like his earlier question (3.1.103)
to Ophelia, "Ha, ha! Are you honest?" Or, on the other hand,
has Hamlet (as in many productions) suddenly glimpsed
Polonius's foot protruding from beneath a drapery at the

rear? That is, does Hamlet ask the question because he has suddenly seen something suspicious and now is testing Ophelia? (By the way, in productions that do give Hamlet a physical cue, it is almost always Polonius rather than Claudius who provides the clue. This itself is an act of interpretation on the part of the director.) Or (a third possibility) does Hamlet get a clue from Ophelia, who inadvertently betrays the spies by nervously glancing at their place of hiding? This is the interpretation used in the BBC television version, where Ophelia glances in fear toward the hiding place just after Hamlet says "Why wouldst thou be a breeder of sinners?" (121–22). Hamlet, realizing that he is being observed, glances here and there *before* he asks "Where's your father?" The question thus is a climax to what he has been doing while speaking the preceding lines. Or (a fourth interpretation) does Hamlet suddenly, without the aid of any clue whatsoever, intuitively (insightfully, mysteriously, wonderfully) sense that someone is spying? Directors must decide, of course—and so must readers.

Recall, too, the preceding discussion of the texts of the plays, which argued that the texts—though they seem to be before us in permanent black on white—are unstable. The Signet text of *Hamlet*, which draws on the Second Quarto (1604) and the First Folio (1623) is considerably longer than any version staged in Shakespeare's time. Our version, even if spoken very briskly and played without any intermission, would take close to four hours, far beyond "the two hours' traffic of our stage" mentioned in the Prologue to *Romeo and Juliet*. (There are a few contemporary references to the duration of a play, but none mentions more than three hours.) Of Shakespeare's plays, only *The Comedy of Errors*, *Macbeth*, and *The Tempest* can be done in less than three hours without cutting. And even if we take a play that exists only in a short text, *Macbeth*, we cannot claim that we are experiencing the very play that Shakespeare conceived, partly because some of the Witches' songs almost surely are non-Shakespearean additions, and partly because we are not willing to watch the play performed without an intermission and with boys in the female roles.

Further, as the earlier discussion of costumes mentioned, the plays apparently were given chiefly in contemporary, that is, in Elizabethan dress. If today we give them in the costumes that Shakespeare probably saw, the plays seem not contemporary but curiously dated. Yet if we use our own dress, we find lines of dialogue that are at odds with what we see; we may feel that the language, so clearly not our own, is inappropriate coming out of people in today's dress. A common solution, incidentally, has been to set the plays in the nineteenth century, on the grounds that this attractively distances the plays (gives them a degree of foreignness, allowing for interesting costumes) and yet doesn't put them into a museum world of Elizabethan England.

Inevitably our productions are adaptations, *our* adaptations, and inevitably they will look dated, not in a century but in twenty years, or perhaps even in a decade. Still, we cannot escape from our own conceptions. As the director Peter Brook has said, in *The Empty Space* (1968):

> It is not only the hair-styles, costumes and make-ups that look dated. All the different elements of staging—the shorthands of behavior that stand for emotions; gestures, gesticulations and tones of voice—are all fluctuating on an invisible stock exchange all the time. . . . A living theatre that thinks it can stand aloof from anything as trivial as fashion will wilt. (p. 16)

As Brook indicates, it is through today's hairstyles, costumes, makeup, gestures, gesticulations, tones of voice— this includes our *conception* of earlier hairstyles, costumes, and so forth if we stage the play in a period other than our own—that we inevitably stage the plays.

It is a truism that every age invents its own Shakespeare, just as, for instance, every age has invented its own classical world. Our view of ancient Greece, a slave-holding society in which even free Athenian women were severely circumscribed, does not much resemble the Victorians' view of ancient Greece as a glorious democracy, just as, perhaps, our view of Victorianism itself does not much resemble theirs. We cannot claim that the Shakespeare on our stage is the true Shakespeare, but in our stage productions we find a Shakespeare that speaks to us, a Shakespeare that our ancestors doubtless did not know but one that seems to us to be the true Shakespeare—at least for a while.

Our age is remarkable for the wide variety of kinds of staging that it uses for Shakespeare, but one development deserves special mention. This is the now common practice of race-blind or color-blind or nontraditional casting, which allows persons who are not white to play in Shakespeare. Previously blacks performing in Shakespeare were limited to a mere three roles, Othello, Aaron (in *Titus Andronicus*), and the Prince of Morocco (in *The Merchant of Venice*), and there were no roles at all for Asians. Indeed, African-Americans rarely could play even one of these three roles, since they were not welcome in white companies. Ira Aldridge (c.1806–1867), a black actor of undoubted talent, was forced to make his living by performing Shakespeare in England and in Europe, where he could play not only Othello but also—in whiteface—other tragic roles such as King Lear. Paul Robeson (1898–1976) made theatrical history when he played Othello in London in 1930, and there was some talk about bringing the production to the United States, but there was more talk about whether American audiences would tolerate the sight of a black man—a real black man, not a white man in blackface—kissing and then killing a white woman. The idea was tried out in summer stock in 1942, the reviews were enthusiastic, and in the following year Robeson opened on Broadway in a production that ran an astounding 296 performances. An occasional all-black company sometimes performed Shakespeare's plays, but otherwise blacks (and other minority members) were in effect shut out from performing Shakespeare. Only since about 1970 has it been common for nonwhites to play major roles along with whites. Thus, in a 1996–97 production of *Antony and Cleopatra*, a white Cleopatra, Vanessa Redgrave, played opposite a black Antony, David Harewood. Multiracial casting is now especially common at the New York Shakespeare Festival, founded in 1954 by Joseph Papp, and in England, where even siblings such as Claudio and Isabella in *Measure for Measure* or Lear's three daughters may be of different races. Probably most viewers today soon stop worrying about the lack of realism, and move beyond the color of the performers' skin to the quality of the performance.

Nontraditional casting is not only a matter of color or race; it includes sex. In the past, occasionally a distinguished woman of the theater has taken on a male role—Sarah Bernhardt (1844–1923) as Hamlet is perhaps the most famous example—but such performances were widely regarded as eccentric. Although today there have been some performances involving cross-dressing (a drag *As You Like It* staged by the National Theatre in England in 1966 and in the United States in 1974 has achieved considerable fame in the annals of stage history), what is more interesting is the casting of women in roles that traditionally are male but that need not be. Thus, a 1993–94 English production of *Henry V* used a woman—*not* cross-dressed—in the role of the governor of Harfleur. According to Peter Holland, who reviewed the production in *Shakespeare Survey* 48 (1995), "having a female Governor of Harfleur feminized the city and provided a direct response to the horrendous threat of rape and murder that Henry had offered, his language and her body in direct connection and opposition" (p. 210). Ten years from now the device may not play so effectively, but today it speaks to us. Shakespeare, born in the Elizabethan Age, has been dead nearly four hundred years, yet he is, as Ben Jonson said, "not of an age but for all time." We must understand, however, that he is "for all time" precisely because each age finds in his abundance something for itself and something of itself.

And here we come back to two issues discussed earlier in this introduction—the instability of the text and, curiously, the Bacon/Oxford heresy concerning the authorship of the plays. *Of course* Shakespeare wrote the plays, and we should daily fall on our knees to thank him for them—and yet there is something to the idea that he is not their only author. Every editor, every director and actor, and every reader to some degree shapes them, too, for when we edit, direct, act, or read, we inevitably become Shakespeare's collaborator and re-create the plays. The plays, one might say, are so cunningly contrived that they guide our responses, tell us how we ought to feel, and make a mark on us, but (for better or for worse) we also make a mark on them.

—SYLVAN BARNET
Tufts University

The First Part of Henry the Sixth

Introduction

The First Part of Henry the Sixth is a play with many imperfections, so many, indeed, that editors and critics have often been reluctant to attribute the greater part of it to Shakespeare. "That Drum-and-trumpet Thing," the eighteenth-century critic Maurice Morgann called it in his essay on Sir John Falstaff, "written doubtless, or rather exhibited, long before *Shakespeare* was born, tho' afterwards repaired, I think, and furbished up by him with here and there a little sentiment and diction."

Such reluctance of ascription has led to the expenditure of much scholarly energy on attempts to isolate as undeniably Shakespearean a few scenes, in particular the finely managed quarrel of the Yorkists and Lancastrians in the Temple Garden (2.4), and to assign the bulk of the work to various teams of collaborators, among them Christopher Marlowe, George Peele, Thomas Nashe, and Robert Greene. Another consequence has been an exceptional tentativeness in much of the critical speculation about *1 Henry VI,* though several fine studies have been made of its significance in Shakespeare's evolution from prentice playwright to master dramatist.

Arguments against Shakespeare's authorship, or primacy within a group of collaborators, have focused mainly upon resemblances in the text to patterns of diction and versification characteristic of other Elizabethan playwrights. The evidence amassed has been considerable, though sometimes contradictory; at times impressive, but never conclusive. For it is likely enough that a Shakespeare who was just setting out on his literary career would have tended to imitate the stylistic mannerisms of already established dramatists. Even Allison Gaw, among the champions of multiple authorship one of the most sensitive to the potential and actual virtues of the play, failed to associate the unusual effort to integrate historical theme and dramatic structure in a theatrically meaningful way with the designing hand of Shakespeare.

Against the collaborationist theory, however, have stood a number of commentators, among them Charles Knight and Hermann Ulrici in the nineteenth century and Peter Alexander, J. P. Brockbank, Leo Kirschbaum, Hereward Price, and E.M.W. Tillyard in our own time. These critics perceive the three dramas on the reign of Henry VI as of one piece, and regard the case for denying the Shakespearean authorship of any part as not proved. It would be rash to assert categorically that *1 Henry VI* as printed in the Folio of 1623 is entirely by Shakespeare, or that no version involving extensive collaboration with others ever did exist. But an approach to the play through the relationship between theme and dramatic design, rather than through its stylistic echoes of various contemporary writers, does considerably strengthen the argument that Shakespeare played the major, if not an exclusive, role in its composition.

Any reader or spectator coming to *1 Henry VI* after exposure to the chronicle plays of other Elizabethan authors is suddenly aware that here he is being asked not simply to observe the pageant of history, but to ponder the meaning of man's role in history. Most other works of the period in this dramatic kind are, even more evidently than the civic and national chronicles upon which they are based, mere strings of episodes in sequence of time, governed, if by any sense of theme at all, by the notion of the capriciousness of the goddess Fortune. Very few are concerned with seeking any other guiding principle in history or with the dramatic interaction of personalities within the pattern of historical events. Very few are concerned with the meaning of history at all, their authors often preferring instead, like a certain kind of modern historical novelist, to invent romantic situations involving historical personages within a bare framework of actual events.

The theme that runs throughout the tetralogy of plays composed by Shakespeare on the reigns of Henry VI and Richard III, and in fact throughout all of his dramatizations of English history, is the individual's, and a people's, response to the continuing alternations of order and disorder allowed by divine providence in the political life of a nation. A strong and heroic king whose regime brings glory and harmony to the commonwealth is succeeded by a monarch lacking, through extreme youth or defect of character, in the virtues necessary for unifying all the diverse constituents of society. The ineptitude or negligence of the sovereign looses the restraints on ambitious and unscrupulous subjects, whose schemes and counterschemes for self-aggrandizement promote faction, public disorder, and eventually civil war. As Tillyard points out in the selections printed later in this volume, in the struggle for domination degree, or acknowledgment of one's proper place in the hierarchically constituted political, and even cosmic, order, is forgotten. "Vaulting ambition" causes men to o'erleap themselves and drag the rest of society with them to the brink of chaos. Finally, when a ruler appears who is powerful and virtuous enough to triumph over the contending parties and restore degree and order, the hallmarks to the Elizabethan mind of good political economy, the wheel comes full circle.

Like the sixteenth-century chronicler Edward Hall, Shakespeare seems, officially at least, to have regarded the larger cycle of order emerging from disorder as having come round fully with the rise of the Tudor dynasty. Hall, whose book is entitled *The Union of the Two Noble and Illustre Families of Lancaster and York,* believed that the cause of the civil warfare which plagued England intermittently throughout the fifteenth century had been removed by the coronation of Henry VIII, whose father was connected with the Lancastrian, or Red-Rose, branch of the royal family, and whose mother was the daughter and heir of the Yorkist, or White-Rose, King Edward IV. For Shakespeare and his contemporaries, the full benefit of this restoration of harmony and degree after the near-anarchy of the Wars of the Roses was manifest in the long and prosperous reign of their virgin queen. "This royal infant," prophesies Archbishop Cranmer of the just-christened Elizabeth in the final scene of *Henry the Eighth,*

Though in her cradle, yet now promises
Upon this land a thousand thousand blessings
Which time shall bring to ripeness.

(5.5.18–20)

Nor will the maiden queen's death, continues Cranmer (how unprophetic the playwright here becomes of later Stuart history!), set the old cycle in motion again, because phoenixlike her "blessedness" will be reborn in her successor.

But Shakespeare was more concerned with presenting the ill effects of disrupted order than with depicting the glories of successful monarchs. Of all his plays on British historical or pseudohistorical subjects, only one, *Henry V,* concentrates on the personality of an all-prosperous ruler and an undeniably glorious moment in England's past. Despite the good fortune of the kingdom during most of Elizabeth's reign, he apparently brooded about the possibility that the cycle might recur, especially if men should ignore the lessons taught by history. Within the larger cycle described by Hall and accepted as complete by many writers of his age, Shakespeare saw smaller cycles or undulations of order and chaos that should have reminded men how precarious any state of equilibrium is in their moral and political lives.

This is not to suggest that in his earliest years as a playwright he had already blocked out in his mind a whole series of dramas to illustrate the pattern and point the historical lessons for his audiences. The order of composition of his various "chronicle histories" should dispel any such assumption. The later-written tetralogy on the troubled history of England toward the end of the Middle Ages—*Richard II, Henry IV: Parts I and II,* and *Henry V*—deals with events that antedate those of the three *Henry VI* plays and *Richard III.* There also exists some possibility that the second and third parts of *Henry VI* were composed before and provided suggestions for the first. Even the earlier tetralogy, therefore, hints at a gradually emerging and changing conception in Shakespeare's mind of what his subject signified and how that significance might be rendered in dramatic terms.

The breakdown of good order, manifest in the undermining of ancient chivalric ideals that had earlier held society together, has its origins for Shakespeare in the events leading to the deposition of King Richard II at the close of the fourteenth century. Richard, a minor at his accession and as an adult deficient in the private and public virtues requisite in a king, is forced to abdicate by his cousin Henry

Bolingbroke, whom he has wronged. Bolingbroke, reigning as King Henry IV, is haunted by the rebellions consequent upon Richard's death; his own success in violating degree has ironically given rise to ambition in others. His son Henry V, however, brings to the throne a clearer conscience and the qualities needed for effective rule. His triumphant kingship marks the close of one of the smaller historical cycles, and is epitomized in his ability to control the anarchical forces in society and weld its different elements into the efficient little army that defeats the French at Agincourt (1415).

Yet this brief period of glory is only an interval in the larger pattern. The hero-king has scotched, not killed, "civil dissension," the "viperous worm / That gnaws the bowels of the commonwealth" (*1 Henry VI,* 3.1.72–73). The opening scene of *1 Henry VI* is shrewdly designed to give warning of the impending disorder. At the funeral of Henry V the four speeches by the king's brothers and uncles convey an awesome sense of cosmic upheaval and heavy finality. Their foreboding is immediately justified, for within less than three dozen lines the lamentations dissolve into a quarrel between the Duke of Gloucester and the Bishop of Winchester. This altercation symbolizes the release of disruptive forces within a society deprived of its main source of unity. Bedford, the new king's uncle, in fact responds to the quarrel with a desperate invocation, asking Henry V's spirit, as his living presence had done, to

Prosper this realm, keep it from civil broils,
Combat with adverse planets in the heavens!

(1.1.53–54)

Nor does the playwright waste any further time before showing how disastrous has been the untimely death of this "king of so much worth." Bedford's prayer is interrupted by the entrance of a courier, who rushes in unceremoniously with news of English reversals in France. He is succeeded by two others, each arriving with worse tidings, worst of all being the account of Lord Talbot's capture. The remarkable economy of the scene is evident from the impact made by this trio of messengers. Their accounts project to the audience the importance for England's success in France of the efforts of such leaders as Salisbury, Talbot, and Bedford, who reacts to the news by preparing to go immediately to the aid of the others. Through this sequence of speeches the dramatist focuses attention on the three warriors, who stand for the ideals that have caused English arms until now to prosper. Yet all three worthy nobles are represented as advanced in years and fated to die later in the play. They carry with them to their graves not only the hopes of England's monarchs for possessing the crown of France, but also the chivalric ideals of a more innocent and masculine era. Their kind will be displaced, at least temporarily, by a self-seeking breed of new "risers," the Winchesters, the Suffolks, and the Yorks.

In spite of Bedford's resolve, there can be no doubt as the scene concludes that all coherence is already gone, that the downturn in England's fortunes has begun. With a real instinct for symmetrical design, the author concludes the scene by repeating the pattern of its opening. The royal brothers and uncles take their leave in precisely the order in which they have been introduced as speakers. As each goes his way to carry out his separate function in governing the realm, there is a momentary feeling that if they can work to one end, all may yet be well. Lest the audience presume, however, that shared grief and determination to act will lead to an effective coalition, the sense of division, of a pilotless ship of state, is emphasized by the words and pageantry of the departures. When all the rest are gone, there remains the unscrupulous politician Winchester, whose earlier altercation with Gloucester has already struck the note of discord, and who regards his nephew's death as an opportunity for him to seize control "And sit at chiefest stern of public weal" (177).

The masterful construction of this introductory scene is more evident in theatrical performance than from silent reading. For it wants, as does the play on the whole, that poetic fire one is accustomed to look for in the work of Shakespeare. But as has often been remarked about his career, he seems to have developed a keen feeling for construction and for what is theatrically right before he evolved a poetic style that can thrill the auditor with its justness for the occasion or discriminate for the sensitive ear subtle differences of mood and character.

Symmetry and purposefulness of design, unlike the form-lessness of most Elizabethan chronicle plays, are indeed the keynotes of this work, and of the Lancaster-York tetralogy as a whole. If later—beginning with *Richard II* and *Henry IV* and at length most impressively in *King Lear* and *Macbeth*—Shakespeare learned to portray characters helping to shape as well as enduring history or growing in perception and self-knowledge from their interaction with events, in *1 Henry VI* he is not yet ready for such an achievement. Here the problem of man's role in history is reduced to simpler terms: a dramatic personage responds in a particular way to events and to other persons involved in the action because he has a fixed character, rather than the possibility of an evolving one. This simple consistency is, in a way, true even of the heroicomical portrayal of Joan of Arc. Although she gives an impression at the outset of being admirably eloquent, efficient, and patriotic, and then of degenerating into wantonness and diabolism, the unsavory side of her character is hinted at in her very first scene. If we are disturbed by the seemingly inconsistent and finally unchivalrous treatment of the Maid of Orleans, we should remind ourselves that in Shakespeare's day she had not yet been canonized or become the subject of more sympathetic characterizations by dramatists like Schiller, Shaw, and Anouilh. Character in Shakespeare's play is conceived broadly, flatly; the peculiar quality of every personage is unequivocally represented.

The solution for him, consequently, was to develop his dramatic theme mainly through formal structure; that is, through symbolically parallel and contrasting episodes, and through confrontations between characters representing sharply defined ethical and political values.

The first clue to this intention is the extremely cavalier handling of chronology, a disruption of time-sequence far beyond that in any of Shakespeare's other plays based on chronicles. Rather than demonstrating an ignorance of history or indifference to order, the rearrangement of events indicates a sense on the author's part that dramatic logic and the historical lesson are better served by recreating than by retelling what happened in the past. Thus, while *1 Henry VI* is grounded upon chronicle materials, it employs them so freely that one is not always certain how much indebted to the sources a given scene may be, or even, except in manifest instances, whether the principal inspiration is the work of Edward Hall or that of Raphael Holinshed.

The play also includes totally fictional scenes, among them the dispute in the Temple Garden and Talbot's encounter with the Countess of Auvergne. Unlike the arbitrarily invented episodes common in other history plays of the age, those in *1 Henry VI* serve to clarify the meaning of actual events, far more effectively than anything available to the author in his historical sources. The disjointing of time, moreover, enables him to achieve striking dramatic and didactic effects. The episodes cover a period of more than thirty years, from the beginning of Henry VI's reign in 1422 to the death of the Talbots near Bordeaux in 1453, but from the opening lines incidents are juxtaposed that were in actuality separated by a number of years. Thus, the siege of Orleans (1428–29) is already taking place during the funeral of Henry V seven years earlier. The dramaturgical reason is evident: to introduce immediately the main conflict, between Joan of France and Talbot of England. In Act 5, the capture of Joan (1430) is succeeded directly and without even a scene division by Suffolk's fictitious capture and wooing of Margaret of Anjou, though the negotiations for the king's marriage did not actually take place until 1444. Finally, the death of the Talbots, chronologically the last in the long series of events here dramatized, precedes these other carefully paired episodes. Apparently this dislocation was made in order to maintain as long as possible the symbolical conflict between the mirror of English chivalry and the diabolically assisted Joan, and also to imply that Margaret is about to arise from Joan's ashes to carry on the scourging of England in the remainder of the trilogy.

Divine providence allows England to be plagued by infernal as well as political enemies because her people have sinned. How the nation might have remained true to itself is signified by the words and deeds of Talbot. What she is in danger of becoming is signified in the shortcomings of the French, failings that crop up increasingly among Englishmen as the action of the play proceeds. The dissension that breaks out at home in the opening lines begins immediately to sap the English strength abroad, for it is accompanied by the decay of feudal loyalties and forgetfulness of degree. Also manifest are an English decline toward French effeminacy and the beginnings of reliance on fraud and cunning rather than manly courage and straightforward knightly virtue.

In the second scene, which shifts to Orleans, the playwright quickly sketches in the defective moral character of Frenchmen, as epitomized in the behavior of the Dauphin. A braggart like his counterpart in Shakespeare's *Henry V,* he begins a sortie against the English with the cry to his followers,

> Him I forgive my death that killeth me
> When he sees me go back one foot or fly.

> (1.2.20–21)

Some moments later, his forces are beaten back, and he excuses his retreat in words a Talbot or a Salisbury would have died rather than utter:

> I would ne'er have fled,
> But that they left me 'midst my enemies.

> (23–24)

Nothing they can do as men, it is apparent from the ensuing conversation among the French leaders, can overcome these dogged Englishmen.

At this point Joan comes onstage, and the Dauphin's conversation with her brings out two grave defects of Frenchmen that also begin gradually to taint the characters of Englishmen in the play. After bowing to her in single combat, Charles woos Joan in the language not of her royal prince, but of the fashionable courtly lover, asking to be her "servant and not sovereign," and imploring her "mercy" (that is, the favor of her love) as her "prostrate thrall." Such domination by the female is obviously scorned by an audience of Tudor Englishmen; it confirms their prejudices against Gallic dandyism and effeminacy. For in spite of Joan's high-sounding claims and self-assertive dash, one's admiration of her must stop far short of the Dauphin's; she is, after all, no more than a shepherd's daughter from Lorraine. The comedy of the scene is also obvious. From the number of double entendres in the Ovidian tradition of love-making as armed combat, the audience can scarcely be expected to take seriously Joan's claims to divine inspiration and vow to maintain her virginity while Englishmen remain on her country's soil.

All doubt about the tenor of the scene is dispelled by Charles's final ecstatic response to her messianic claims:

> Was Mahomet inspirèd with a dove?
> Thou with an eagle art inspirèd then.
> Helen, the mother of great Constantine,
> Nor yet Saint Philip's daughters, were like thee.
> Bright star of Venus, fall'n down on the earth,
> How may I reverently worship thee enough?
>
>   (140–45)

Not only are the allusions to other lofty examples of divine inspiration too characteristic of the Dauphin's lack of moderation to be taken seriously, but their very extravagance is a strong hint that Joan's pretensions are false. When Charles climaxes his apostrophe with the words "Bright star of Venus," the imagery of courtly wooing and the bawdy overtones of the earlier part of the scene intrude themselves again. Besides, "star of Venus, fall'n down on the earth," calls to mind not only the goddess of profane love, but also Lucifer, that brightest of angelic stars tumbled out of the heavens for his aspiration to divinity. Feminine wiles are thus linked by the epithet with diabolical fraud and deception. Charles is blameworthy for allowing himself to be dominated by a woman—a peasant girl at that!—and for resorting to preternatural aid in his efforts to rid his country of the English. "Coward of France!" exclaims Bedford,

>   how much he wrongs his fame,
> Despairing of his own arm's fortitude,
> To join with witches and the help of hell.
>
>   (2.1.16–18)

The rest of the scenes in France are fashioned to contrast the reprehensible behavior of Joan and the Dauphin, as well as of Englishmen whose characters become similarly stained as the moral fiber of their leaderless country weakens, with that of the upright Talbot. These contrasts are effectively brought out through patterns, as Ernest Talbert calls them, of "intensified repetition." One such pattern is the strategic paralleling of episodes either to heighten the opposition between worthy and reprehensible forms of behavior or to point up symbolical relationships between apparently unconnected incidents. The playwright is also fond of grouping characters and episodes in climactic triads to underscore several of the main themes of the play.

Thus, since Talbot is the standard by which the measure of the other characters is taken, his first meeting with Henry VI is presented as an idealized interview between an unselfishly devoted vassal and his sovereign. For his loyal service and recovery in France of

> fifty fortresses,
> Twelve cities, and seven wallèd towns of strength,
> Beside five hundred prisoners of esteem,
>
> (3.4.6–8)

Talbot is created Earl of Shrewsbury. But the episode distinctly recalls the first scene of the same act, where the already scheming Plantagenet is made Duke of York without having done anything to merit his elevation and pledges his fealty to the king with a hollow heart. Again, in the opening scene of Act 4 Talbot tears the Garter from Falstaff's* leg for cowardice in battle and delivers a speech on what it means to bear "the sacred name of knight" (4.1.40). His action is a clear example of how noblemen, in helping the monarch to maintain true order and degree, should deal with the presumptions of their subordinates.

As soon as Talbot departs, however, Vernon and Basset disrupt the coronation scene with their demands for trial by combat in behalf of their respective masters, York and Somerset. In order to further their own ambitions, Henry's nobles are obviously willing to let faction breed rather than suppress their contentious retainers. Toward the end of the scene York even appears to be on the point of exclaiming

---

*Not the famous fat knight of *Henry IV*, whose death is described in *Henry V*, but rather a character based on the historical Sir John Fastolfe (*c.*1378–1459), a prominent retainer of the Duke of Bedford and, according to the chronicles, one of the most valiant captains in the regent's armies.

to Warwick (line 180) that he would prefer to have the king himself take sides against him since he might then turn it to his own advantage. This is but one of several scenes in which Talbot's conduct is sharply contrasted with that of other characters. The dramatist's intentions are unmistakable: Talbot is the ideal, the centripetal force of order that gradually gives way to the centrifugal forces of chaos represented by York and others of the rising new breed.

Dramatic triads appear in many places in *1 Henry VI* from the opening scene onward: the sense of climactic urgency in the arrival of the three messengers hot on one another's heels; the trio of ambitious nobles—Winchester, York, Suffolk; the focusing on the three stout but aging generals—Salisbury, Bedford, and Talbot—each of whose deaths is a more discouraging blow, the last the final blow, to English dynastic ambitions in France. Talbot opposes the French and their sorceress champion on all three of these occasions: at Orleans, where Salisbury is shot; at Rouen, where Bedford dies; and finally near Bordeaux, where he and his son meet their heroic end.

In each incident, fraud at first succeeds, not force of arms, and the placing of blame in each indicates progressive deterioration on the English side. At Orleans, Salisbury is killed by chance and Talbot is temporarily set back, to his complete bewilderment, by Joan's "art and baleful sorcery" (2.1.15). His martial enterprise and trust in God, however, in contrast with the Frenchmen's lax discipline and reliance on "the help of hell" (18), win the day for him when he returns to the attack. At Rouen (3.2) Joan gains entrance by means of a stratagem historically employed by the English on another occasion, according to Holinshed, and transferred in the play to the French as an instance of their treachery. Eventually, Talbot overcomes again, while Bedford watches the struggle from "his litter sick" (95). But now it is not only the French who are cowardly, who, as Talbot complains,

> keep the walls
> And dare not take up arms like gentlemen.

>   (69–70)

Just before the victory is assured and Bedford dies content, Falstaff again shows the white feather, this time on stage instead of in a messenger's report, and runs like a Frenchman from the battle scene. It is this defection that provides the occasion for Talbot later to tear the badge of the Order of the Garter from his leg at Henry's coronation in Paris.

At Bordeaux, where the audience might expect a final confrontation between Talbot and Joan, none is provided, nor does Joan make use of any cunning device to gain advantage over the English. The dramatist's reasons are clear enough. They are placed in the mouth of Sir William Lucy as he vainly begs York and Somerset to come to Talbot's relief. It is "the vulture of sedition" (4.3.47) and "Sleeping neglection" (49) that are causing the loss of Henry V's conquests:

> The fraud of England, not the force of France,
> Hath now entrapped the noble-minded Talbot.
>
> (4.4.36–37)

Malice and cunning deceit are beginning to corrupt even the highest English nobility, and Talbot is the sacrifice to their dissension. Yet even against the forces of hell and the wily allurements of womankind, England might have stood fast, if only all her noblemen had been like her stoutest champion. But when men place their self-interest ahead of the common good, the old ideals are readily forgotten. Joan's cunning becomes no longer necessary; the English are now their own worst enemies, having succumbed to the vices of the French.

This eroding of English virtue is nowhere more skillfully depicted than in the triad of scenes involving the first appearances of each of the three evil-designing Frenchwomen (interestingly enough, the only feminine characters in the play!). The scenes in question are Joan's introduction to the Dauphin, Talbot's reception by the Countess of Auvergne (2.3), and Suffolk's wooing of Margaret of Anjou (5.3). All three women represent a threat to English fortunes; the manner in which the three men respond to them neatly dramatizes the lesson.

Earlier it was pointed out that not only the Dauphin's accepting the demonically inspired assistance of Joan, but also his self-debasement to servant-lover of a peasant girl, is conduct inexcusable in a prince. And even if his behavior were not a burlesque of courtly traditions, it runs counter to the ruggedly heroic ideal represented by Talbot. Not that

Talbot is a boor: he does know how to treat a lady as becomes a worthy English chevalier. The Dauphin's involvement with Joan is a breaking of degree and serves, moreover, to unhinge her judgment of herself even beyond what traffic with fiends has done. When she is finally on her way to the stake, this peasant maiden who has been graced with sovereignty over her infatuated monarch pretends to "noble birth" and "gentler blood" than that of her shepherd father. Even the phrase with which she rejects the old man—"Decrepit miser!"—accentuates her disdain for her lowly origins; *miser* is the worst term of opprobrium in the vocabulary of the courtly tradition.

But the true measure of the Dauphin's folly is the scene between Talbot and the fictional Countess. This lady too plots evil to the English through her ruse for capturing "the terror of the French." There is even a suggestion that she, like Joan, may have resorted to witchcraft by practicing sympathetic magic on her guest's portrait:

> Long time thy shadow hath been thrall to me,
> For in my gallery thy picture hangs.
> But now the substance shall endure the like.

(2.3.36–38)

The resourceful Talbot, however, outwits her by a simple counterstratagem and, refusing like a true and valiant gentleman to avenge himself on so weak an adversary, asks only honest entertainment for himself and his men before they take their leave.

Obviously if all of Talbot's compatriots had been thus immune to the allure of scheming Frenchwomen, all might have remained well enough for England. But the third encounter of this kind, that between Suffolk and Reignier's daughter Margaret, shows that Englishmen no longer are men of true honor, who, in contrast with the French, place their country's interests above their own selfish desires. Suffolk is dazzled, almost bewitched, by Margaret's beauty when he first gazes on her. And while he is the active, she almost entirely the passive, agent in this scene, from the course taken by the remaining action there can be little doubt that this woman will supplant Joan as the punishment for the sins of faction and ambition among Englishmen. Having Joan's and Margaret's captures occur in the same scene, in another of those symbolically meaningful parallelings of seemingly unconnected episodes, is theatrically most effective. And even though Joan's final scenes are far different in tone from Margaret's entry into the action, they serve a twofold function in helping to knit up the events of *1 Henry VI* and to anticipate the subsequent development of the trilogy.

In defiance of historical fact, but with excellent dramatic sense, York is made to be Joan's captor and judge. But even as he is mercilessly taunting his prisoner about her past affairs with the Dauphin and his nobles, another game of man and woman is being played that will prove his undoing. The parting curses of Joan are not the impotent ragings of a "Fell banning hag" (5.3.42); they are prophecies of ambitious York's own downfall and of the miserable years for England that are being engendered in the dalliance of Suffolk with Margaret of Anjou.

Suffolk would enjoy this lady's love and use her to further his own ends at the sacrifice of English interests in France. Worse still, his "wondrous rare description" (5.5.1) of Margaret's beauty serves to corrupt King Henry's mind and causes him to break his pre-contract of marriage with the daughter of the Earl of Armagnac. That the choice is both impolitic and immoral is clear from the king's own inner turmoil in the last moments of the play: the "sharp dissension" (84) that he feels within makes him "sick with working of my thoughts" (86), and he finally departs in a state of "grief" (101) rather than expectant elation at "This sudden execution of my will" (99).

The threat latent in Henry's impending marriage to Margaret, with whose arrival in England the second part of the trilogy opens, is brilliantly suggested by a pair of images in the last scene of Part One. The king compares his infatuation to a tempest, driving his soul against its more settled inclinations like a ship against the tide:

> So am I driven by breath of her renown
> Either to suffer shipwreck or arrive
> Where I may have fruition of her love.

> (7–9)

The sudden intrusion here of the conventional figure of the lover as a vessel in danger of shipwreck on the stormy seas of passion calls to mind the dangers that Petrarch *("Passa la nave mia colma d'oblio")* and his imitator Sir Thomas Wyatt ("My galley chargèd with forgetfulness") lamented as besetting the soul of the man tossed by sexual desire. For a king to make such an admission, and then to overrule good counsel and follow the inclination of his will rather than reasons of state, is a most unregal kind of behavior.

Most disturbing of all, however, are the verses with which the drama concludes. If restoration of order were to be implied at the end of the action, according to the usual Shakespearean closing formula there would be a speech explicitly saying so. But here the final words, coming after the king's confused withdrawal, are left for Suffolk, who exults in his success and departs for Anjou

> As did the youthful Paris once to Greece,
> With hope to find the like event in love,
> But prosper better than the Trojan did.

> (104–106)

The image could hardly be lost on an Elizabethan audience, whose own mythmaking historians traced the ancestry of the British race to Troy. French Margaret will bring disaster to England as certainly as Spartan Helen brought ruin to "the topless towers of Ilium."

The remainder of the trilogy portrays Margaret, though she is in neither play the solely dominating figure, as an evil influence in England's domestic affairs. In Part Two it is she and her lover Suffolk, along with the malevolent Winchester, who engineer the downfall of the Duke of Gloucester. In Part Three, her monstrous treatment of her archrival York is the climax of her role as England's scourge. Eventually, in *Richard III,* this figure of nemesis who for long has borne a "tiger's heart wrapped in a woman's hide," becomes inactive though not silent, an unheeded Cassandra warning the now-dominant House of York of its own impending doom.

Though not a great poetic drama, *1 Henry VI* is by no means a failure as a play for theatrical performance. It

exhibits a thoughtful design through which important themes
are vigorously, if somewhat crudely, realized in the com-
pleted action. Nor is the affair of Margaret and Suffolk, as
some critics would have it, only an afterthought. Strange as
the final act and scene divisions in the Folio may be, the
matter of these last episodes is not something inexpertly
tacked onto what was originally conceived as an indepen-
dent tragedy of Talbot simply because the author, or reviser,
needed a way to patch together a trilogy. All that previously
transpires is too carefully articulated with the concluding
scenes for that. Act 5 is the logical conclusion to the events
set in motion at the play's beginning, and at the same time
an effective opening-out to the even greater disorder and
calamities of Parts Two and Three. The close is nearly symmetrical with the opening, and far more ominous though
more restrained and economical in its language. A nation
that is leaderless because its king is an infant as the play
begins, is still leaderless, or subject to dangerous misguid-
ance, as the action ends because its now-grown king has succumbed to a destructive passion. And the unscrupulous new
risers have now found an instrument for gaining the illicit
power to which they aspire.

   The bad news from Orleans that marked the downturn of
England's fortunes in France is superseded by bad news
from Angers that will lead to misery on England's soil itself.
All this the maker of *1 Henry VI* was capable of rendering
theatrically effective. By 1592 Shakespeare may not yet
have been a supreme dramatic craftsman, but neither was he
a mere botcher of other men's work, a snapper-up of other
playwrights' unconsidered trifles.

                                        —LAWRENCE V. RYAN

THE HOUSES OF LANCASTER AND YORK
(Simplified)
Edward III (1327–77)

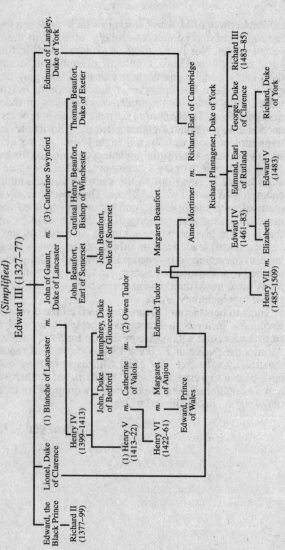

The First Part of Henry the Sixth

[*Dramatis Personae*

King Henry the Sixth
Humphrey, Duke of Gloucester, uncle to the King, and Protector
John, Duke of Bedford, uncle to the King, and Regent of France
Thomas Beaufort, Duke of Exeter, great-uncle to the King
Henry Beaufort, Bishop of Winchester, and afterwards Cardinal, great-uncle to the King
John Beaufort, Earl, afterwards Duke, of Somerset
Richard Plantagenet, afterwards Duke of York, son of Richard, late Earl of Cambridge
Earl of Warwick
Earl of Salisbury
William de la Pole, Earl of Suffolk
Lord Talbot, afterwards Earl of Shrewsbury
John Talbot, Lord Lisle, his son
Edmund Mortimer, Earl of March
Sir John Falstaff*
Sir William Lucy
Sir William Glansdale
Sir Thomas Gargrave
Mayor of London
Woodville, Lieutenant of the Tower
Vernon, of the White-Rose or York faction
Basset, of the Red-Rose or Lancaster faction
A Lawyer. Mortimer's Jailers. A papal Legate

Charles, Dauphin, and afterwards King, of France
Reignier, Duke of Anjou, and titular King of Naples
Duke of Burgundy

*See note, Introduction, p. 13.

Duke of Alençon
Bastard of Orleans
Governor of Paris
Master-Gunner of Orleans, and his Son
General of the French forces in Bordeaux
A French Sergeant. A Porter
An old Shepherd, father to Joan la Pucelle

Margaret, daughter to Reignier, afterwards married to
  King Henry
Countess of Auvergne
Joan la Pucelle, commonly called Joan of Arc

Lords, Ambassadors, Warders of the Tower, Heralds,
  Officers, Soldiers, Messengers, Attendants

Fiends appearing to La Pucelle

Scene: England; France]

ACT 1

Scene 1. [*Westminster Abbey.*]

Dead March.°[1] *Enter the Funeral of King Henry the Fifth, attended on by the Duke of Bedford, Regent of France; the Duke of Gloucester, Protector; the Duke of Exeter, Warwick, the Bishop of Winchester, and the Duke of Somerset, [with Attendants].*

Bedford. Hung be the heavens with black,° yield day
    to night!
  Comets, importing change of times and states,°
  Brandish your crystal° tresses in the sky,
  And with them scourge the bad revolting stars
  That have consented unto° Henry's death!   *5*
  King Henry the Fifth, too famous to live long!
  England ne'er lost a king of so much worth.

---

[1]The degree sign (°) indicates a footnote, which is keyed to the text by line number. Text references are printed in **boldface** type; the annotation follows in roman type.
1.1.s.d. **Dead March** a solemn piece of music for a funeral procession 1 **black** i.e., as a stage was draped in black for a tragedy 2 **Comets . . . states** i.e., the appearance of comets portending some misfortune 3 **crystal** bright 5 **consented unto** conspired to bring about

Gloucester. England ne'er had a king until his time.
     Virtue he had, deserving to command;
     His brandished sword did blind men with his°
10   beams;
     His arms spread wider than a dragon's wings;
     His sparkling eyes, replete with wrathful fire,
     More dazzled and drove back his enemies
     Than midday sun fierce bent against their faces.
15   What should I say? His deeds exceed all speech:
     He ne'er lift° up his hand but conquerèd.

Exeter. We mourn in black; why mourn we not in
          blood?°
     Henry is dead and never shall revive.
     Upon a wooden° coffin we attend,
20   And death's dishonorable victory
     We with our stately presence glorify,
     Like captives bound to a triumphant car.°
     What! shall we curse the planets of mishap°
     That plotted thus our glory's overthrow?
25   Or shall we think the subtle-witted French
     Conjurers and sorcerers that, afraid of him,
     By magic verses have contrived his end?

Winchester. He was a king blessed of the King of
          Kings.
     Unto the French the dreadful judgment day
30   So dreadful will not be as was his sight.
     The battles of the Lord of Hosts he fought;
     The church's prayers made him so prosperous.

Gloucester. The church! Where is it? Had not church-
          men prayed,
     His thread of life had not so soon decayed.
35   None do you like but an effeminate prince,
     Whom, like a schoolboy, you may overawe.

---

10 **his** its   16 **lift** lifted   17 **in blood** i.e., by shedding blood, probably of the French in order to avenge the king's death (see lines
25–27)   19 **wooden** unfeeling   22 **car** chariot   23 **of mishap** causing misfortune

Winchester. Gloucester, whate'er we like, thou art
     Protector°
And lookest° to command the prince and realm.
Thy wife is proud; she holdeth thee in awe
More than God or religious churchmen may.   40

Gloucester. Name not religion, for thou lov'st the
     flesh,
And ne'er throughout the year to church thou go'st
Except it be to pray against thy foes.

Bedford. Cease, cease these jars° and rest your minds
     in peace;
Let's to the altar. Heralds, wait on us.   45
Instead of gold, we'll offer up our arms,°
Since arms avail not now that Henry's dead.
Posterity, await for wretched years,
When at their mothers' moistened eyes babes shall
     suck,
Our isle be made a nourish° of salt tears,   50
And none but women left to wail the dead.
Henry the Fifth, thy ghost I invocate:
Prosper this realm, keep it from civil broils,°
Combat with adverse planets in the heavens!
A far more glorious star thy soul will make   55
Than Julius Caesar° or bright—

Enter a Messenger.

Messenger. My honorable lords, health to you all!
Sad tidings bring I to you out of France,
Of loss, of slaughter, and discomfiture:
Guienne, Champagne, Rheims, Orleans,   60
Paris, Guysors, Poictiers, are all quite lost.

Bedford. What say'st thou, man, before dead Henry's
     corse?°

---

37 **Protector** governor of the realm during the king's minority   38
lookest expect   44 **jars** quarrels   46 **arms** weapons   50 **nourish**
nurse   53 **broils** disorders   56 **Julius Caesar** (whose soul, according to Ovid, *Metamorphoses*, xv. 843–51, became a star in the
heavens after his assassination)   62 **corse** corpse

Speak softly, or the loss of those great towns
Will make him burst his lead° and rise from death.

65 *Gloucester.* Is Paris lost? Is Rouen yielded up?
If Henry were recalled to life again,
These° news would cause him once more yield the
ghost.

Exeter. How were they lost? What treachery was
used?

Messenger. No treachery, but want of men and
money.

70 Amongst the soldiers this is mutterèd,
That here you maintain several factions,°
And whilst a field should be dispatched and fought,
You are disputing of your generals:
One would have ling'ring wars with little cost;

75 Another would fly swift, but wanteth wings;
A third thinks, without expense at all,
By guileful fair words peace may be obtained.
Awake, awake, English nobility!
Let not sloth dim your honors new begot;°

80 Cropped are the flower-de-luces° in your arms;
Of England's coat° one half is cut away.

Exeter. Were our tears wanting° to this funeral,
These tidings would call forth her° flowing tides.

Bedford. Me they concern; Regent° I am of France.

85 Give me my steelèd coat; I'll fight for France.
Away with these disgraceful wailing robes!
Wounds will I lend the French, instead of eyes,
To weep their intermissive° miseries.

64 **lead** lining of the coffin   67 **These** (since *news* was originally plural)   71 **factions** (trisyllabic; the endings *-ion* and *-ions* are often pronounced as two syllables in Shakespeare)   79 **new begot** recently obtained   80 **flower-de-luces** fleur-de-lis, or lilies of France (heraldic symbol of the French monarchs)   81 **coat** coat of arms (the English royal family, as a sign of its pretensions to the throne of France, included the fleur-de-lis in its coat of arms from the fourteenth through the eighteenth centuries)   82 **wanting** lacking   83 **her** i.e., England's   84 **Regent** ruler in the king's absence   88 **intermissive** coming at intervals

Enter to them another Messenger.

Second Messenger. Lords, view these letters full of
   bad mischance.
  France is revolted from the English quite,   90
  Except some petty towns of no import.°
  The Dolphin° Charles is crownèd king in Rheims;
  The Bastard of Orleans with him is joined;
  Reignier, Duke of Anjou, doth take his part;
  The Duke of Alençon flieth to his side.   *Exit.* 95

Exeter. The Dolphin crownèd king? All fly to him?
  O, whither shall we fly from this reproach?°

Gloucester. We will not fly, but to our enemies'
   throats.
  Bedford, if thou be slack, I'll fight it out.

Bedford. Gloucester, why doubt'st thou of my for-
   wardness?   100
  An army have I mustered in my thoughts,
  Wherewith already France is overrun.

Enter another Messenger.

Third Messenger. My gracious lords, to add to your
   laments,
  Wherewith you now bedew° King Henry's hearse,
  I must inform you of a dismal fight   105
  Betwixt the stout Lord Talbot and the French.

Winchester. What? Wherein Talbot overcame, is't so?

Third Messenger. O no, wherein Lord Talbot was
   o'erthrown.
  The circumstance I'll tell you more at large.°
  The tenth of August last, this dreadful lord,   110
  Retiring from the siege of Orleans,
  Having full° scarce six thousand in his troop,

---

91 **import** importance   92 **Dolphin** Dauphin, title of the heir to
the French throne   97 **reproach** disgrace   104 **bedew** moisten
109 **The circumstance . . . large** I shall tell you the details at greater
length   112 **full** all told (?)

By three and twenty thousand of the French
Was round encompassèd and set upon.
115 No leisure had he to enrank° his men;
He wanted pikes° to set before his archers;
Instead whereof, sharp stakes plucked out of hedges
They pitchèd in the ground confusedly,
To keep the horsemen off° from breaking in.
120 More than three hours the fight continuèd;
Where valiant Talbot, above human thought,
Enacted wonders with his sword and lance.
Hundreds he sent to hell, and none durst stand him;
Here, there, and everywhere, enraged he slew.
125 The French exclaimed the devil was in arms;
All the whole army stood agazed° on him.
His soldiers, spying his undaunted spirit,
"A Talbot! a Talbot!" cried out amain,°
And rushed into the bowels of the battle.
130 Here had the conquest fully been sealed up,
If Sir John Falstaff had not played the coward.
He, being in the vanward,° placed behind
With purpose to relieve and follow them,
Cowardly fled, not having struck one stroke.
135 Hence grew the general wrack and massacre:
Enclosèd were they with their enemies.
A base Walloon,° to win the Dolphin's grace,
Thrust Talbot with a spear into the back,
Whom all France, with their chief assembled
     strength,
140 Durst not presume to look once in the face.

Bedford. Is Talbot slain then? I will slay myself
For living idly here in pomp and ease
Whilst such a worthy leader, wanting aid,
Unto his dastard foemen is betrayed.

115 **enrank** set in ranks   116 **pikes** stakes with sharpened iron
points, set in the ground to impale the enemy's horses if the
mounted troops charged the archers   119 **off** (apparently redundant, and inserted for metrical purposes)   126 **agazed** astounded
(probably a variant of *aghast*)   128 **amain** with all their might
132 **vanward** vanguard   137 **Walloon** inhabitant of the region
between northeastern France and the Netherlands

Third Messenger. O no, he lives, but is took prisoner,   *145*
    And Lord Scales with him and Lord Hungerford;
    Most of the rest slaughtered or took likewise.

Bedford. His ransom there is none but I shall pay.
    I'll hale the Dolphin headlong from his throne;
    His crown shall be the ransom of my friend;   *150*
    Four of their lords I'll change for one of ours.
    Farewell, my masters, to my task will I;
    Bonfires in France forthwith I am to make
    To keep our great Saint George's feast° withal.°
    Ten thousand soldiers with me I will take,   *155*
    Whose bloody deeds shall make all Europe quake.

Third Messenger. So you had need, for Orleans is be-
    sieged;
    The English army is grown weak and faint;
    The Earl of Salisbury craveth supply
    And hardly keeps his men from mutiny   *160*
    Since they, so few, watch such a multitude.

Exeter. Remember, lords, your oaths to Henry sworn:
    Either to quell° the Dolphin utterly
    Or bring him in obedience to your yoke.

Bedford. I do remember it and here take my leave   *165*
    To go about my preparation.°   *Exit Bedford.*

Gloucester. I'll to the Tower° with all the haste I can
    To view th' artillery and munition,
    And then I will proclaim young Henry king.
                      Exit Gloucester.

Exeter. To Eltham will I, where the young king is,   *170*
    Being ordained his special governor,
    And for his safety there I'll best devise.   *Exit.*

Winchester. Each hath his place and function to at-
    tend;
    I am left out; for me nothing remains.

154 **Saint George's feast** April 23   154 **withal** with   163 **quell** destroy   166 **preparation** (five syllables)   167 **Tower** Tower of London

175   But long I will not be Jack out of office.°
        The king from Eltham I intend to send
        And sit at chiefest stern of public weal.°

                            Exit [*with Attendants*].

                [Scene 2. *France. Before Orleans.*]

            Sound a Flourish.° Enter Charles [*the Dauphin*],
            Alençon, and Reignier, marching with Drum and
                            Soldiers.

Dauphin. Mars his° true moving, even as in the
            heavens,
        So in the earth, to this day is not known.
        Late did he shine upon the English side;
        Now we are victors; upon us he smiles.
5   What towns of any moment° but we have?
        At pleasure here we lie near Orleans;
        Otherwhiles° the famished English, like pale ghosts,
        Faintly besiege us one hour in a month.

Alençon. They want their porridge and their fat bull-
            beeves:°
10   Either they must be dieted° like mules
        And have their provender° tied to their mouths,
        Or piteous they will look, like drownèd mice.

Reignier. Let's raise the siege; why live we idly here?
        Talbot is taken, whom we wont° to fear;
15   Remaineth none but mad-brained Salisbury,

175 **Jack out of office** a person deprived of official function   177
And . . . weal and maintain control of the government   1.2.s.d.
Flourish fanfare of trumpets   1 **Mars his** Mars's   5 **moment** importance   7 **Otherwhiles** at times   9 **bull-beeves** (eating of bull-
beef was believed to give one courage)   10 **dieted** fed   11 **prov-
ender** food   14 **wont** were accustomed

And he may well in fretting spend his gall;°
Nor° men nor money hath he to make war.

Dauphin. Sound, sound alarum!° we will rush on
  them.
  Now for the honor of the forlorn French!
  Him I forgive my death that killeth me   20
  When he sees me go back one foot or fly.   *Exeunt.*

*Here alarum; they are beaten back by the English with
  great loss. Enter Charles [the Dauphin], Alençon,
  and Reignier.*

Dauphin. Who ever saw the like? What men have I?
  Dogs! cowards! dastards! I would ne'er have fled,
  But that they left me 'midst my enemies.

Reignier. Salisbury is a desperate homicide;   25
  He fighteth as one weary of his life.
  The other lords, like lions wanting food,
  Do rush upon us as their hungry prey.°

Alençon. Froissart,° a countryman of ours, records
  England all Olivers and Rowlands° bred   30
  During the time Edward the Third did reign.
  More truly now may this be verified,
  For none but Samsons and Goliases°
  It sendeth forth to skirmish. One to ten!
  Lean raw-boned rascals!° who would e'er suppose   35
  They had such courage and audacity?

Dauphin. Let's leave this town, for they are
  hare-brained slaves,
  And hunger will enforce° them to be more eager.°
  Of old I know them; rather with their teeth
  The walls they'll tear down than forsake the siege.   40

18 **gall** bitterness of spirit 17 **Nor** neither · 18 **alarum** call to arms
28 **their hungry prey** prey for which they hunger 29 **Froissart** chronicler of fourteenth-century French, English, and Spanish affairs 30
Olivers and Rowlands heroes of the French medieval epic, *La Chan-
son de Roland* 33 **Goliases** Goliaths 35 **rascals** lean, inferior deer
38 **enforce** compel 38 **eager** (1) hungry (2) fierce

Reignier. I think, by some odd gimmors° or device
 Their arms are set, like clocks, still to strike on;
 Else ne'er could they hold out so as they do.
 By my consent, we'll even let them alone.

45 *Alençon.* Be it so.

   Enter the Bastard of Orleans.

Bastard. Where's the Prince Dolphin? I have news
 for him.

Dauphin. Bastard of Orleans, thrice welcome to us.

Bastard. Methinks your looks are sad, your cheer
 appaled.°
 Hath the late overthrow wrought this offense?
50 Be not dismayed, for succor is at hand:
 A holy maid hither with me I bring,
 Which by a vision sent to her from heaven
 Ordainèd is to raise this tedious siege
 And drive the English forth° the bounds of France.
55 The spirit of deep prophecy she hath,
 Exceeding the nine sibyls° of old Rome:
 What's past and what's to come she can descry.
 Speak, shall I call her in? Believe my words,
 For they are certain and unfallible.°

Dauphin. Go, call her in. [*Exit Bastard.*] But first, to
60 try her skill,
 Reignier, stand thou as Dolphin in my place;
 Question her proudly; let thy looks be stern:
 By this means shall we sound° what skill she hath.

  Enter [the Bastard of Orleans, with] Joan [la]
     Pucelle.°

Reignier. Fair maid, is't thou wilt do these wondrous
 feats?

---

41 **gimmors** (variant of *gimmals*) connecting parts for transmitting
motion 48 **cheer appaled** countenance pale with fear 54 **forth**
beyond 56 **nine sibyls** nine books of prophetic utterances offered
to King Tarquin of Rome by the sibyl at Cumae 59 **unfallible**
infallible 63 **sound** test 63s.d. **la Pucelle** the virgin

Pucelle. Reignier, is't thou that thinkest to beguile me?   *65*
    Where is the Dolphin? Come, come from behind;
    I know thee well, though never seen before.
    Be not amazed, there's nothing hid from me;
    In private will I talk with thee apart.
    Stand back, you lords, and give us leave awhile.   *70*

Reignier. She takes upon her bravely at first dash.°

Pucelle. Dolphin, I am by birth a shepherd's daughter,
    My wit° untrained in any kind of art.
    Heaven and our Lady° gracious hath it pleased
    To shine on my contemptible estate.   *75*
    Lo, whilst I waited on my tender lambs,
    And to sun's parching heat displayed my cheeks,
    God's mother deignèd to appear to me
    And in a vision full of majesty
    Willed me to leave my base vocation°   *80*
    And free my country from calamity.
    Her aid she promised and assured success;
    In complete glory she revealed herself;
    And, whereas I was black and swart° before,
    With those clear rays which she infused° on me   *85*
    That beauty am I blessed with which you may see.
    Ask me what question thou canst possible,
    And I will answer unpremeditated;
    My courage try by combat, if thou dar'st,
    And thou shalt find that I exceed my sex.   *90*
    Resolve on this,° thou shalt be fortunate
    If thou receive me for thy warlike mate.°

Dauphin. Thou hast astonished me with thy high
     terms;°
    Only this proof I'll of thy valor make,
    In single combat thou shalt buckle° with me,   *95*
    And if thou vanquishest, thy words are true;
    Otherwise I renounce all confidence.

71 **She . . . dash** she acts bravely at the first encounter   73 **wit** mind
74 **our Lady** the Virgin Mary   80 **vocation** occupation   84 **swart**
dark-complexioned   85 **infused** shed   91 **Resolve on this** be assured of this   92 **mate** (1) comrade (2) sweetheart (?)   93 **high
terms** i.e., mastery of the grand rhetorical style   95 **buckle** (1)
grapple (2) embrace as lovers

Pucelle. I am prepared: here is my keen-edged sword,
    Decked with fine flower-de-luces on each side,
    The which at Touraine, in Saint Katherine's
100   churchyard,
    Out of a great deal of old iron I chose forth.

Dauphin. Then come, a° God's name, I fear no
    woman.

Pucelle. And while I live, I'll ne'er fly from a man.

    Here they fight, and Joan la Pucelle overcomes.

Dauphin. Stay, stay thy hands! thou art an Amazon
105   And fightest with the sword of Deborah.°

Pucelle. Christ's mother helps me, else I were too
    weak.

Dauphin. Whoe'er helps thee, 'tis thou that must help
    me:
    Impatiently I burn with thy desire;
    My heart and hands thou hast at once subdued.
110   Excellent Pucelle, if thy name be so,°
    Let me thy servant° and not sovereign be;
    'Tis the French Dolphin sueth to° thee thus.

Pucelle. I must not yield to any rites of love,
    For my profession's sacred from above;
115   When I have chasèd all thy foes from hence,
    Then will I think upon a recompense.

Dauphin. Meantime look gracious on thy prostrate
    thrall.°

Reignier. My lord, methinks, is very long in talk.

Alençon. Doubtless he shrives this woman to her
    smock;°
120   Else ne'er could he so long protract his speech.

---

102 **a** in   105 **Deborah** prophetess who delivered Israel from oppression by the Canaanites (Judges 4–5)   110 **if thy name be so**
if you really are a virgin   111 **servant** lover   112 **sueth to** woos
117 **thrall** slave   119 **shrives . . . smock** (1) questions her closely
(2) hears her confession to the most minute detail

Reignier. Shall we disturb him, since he keeps no
    mean?°

Alençon. He may mean more than we poor men do
    know:
  These women are shrewd tempters with their
    tongues.

Reignier. My lord, where are you? What devise you
    on?°
  Shall we give o'er Orleans, or no?   125

Pucelle. Why, no, I say, distrustful recreants!°
  Fight till the last gasp; I'll be your guard.

Dauphin. What she says I'll confirm: we'll fight it out.

Pucelle. Assigned am I to be the English scourge.
  This night the siege assuredly I'll raise;   130
  Expect Saint Martin's summer,° halcyon's days,°
  Since I have enterèd into these wars.
  Glory is like a circle in the water,
  Which never ceaseth to enlarge itself
  Till by broad spreading it disperse to nought.   135
  With Henry's death the English circle ends;
  Dispersèd are the glories it included.
  Now am I like that proud insulting° ship
  Which Caesar and his fortune bare° at once.

Dauphin. Was Mahomet inspirèd with a dove?   140
  Thou with an eagle° art inspirèd then.
  Helen,° the mother of great Constantine,
  Nor yet Saint Philip's daughters,° were like thee.

---

121 **keeps no mean** does not control himself   124 **devise you on**
are you deliberating   126 **recreants** cowards   131 **Saint Martin's
summer** Indian summer (named after the feast of Saint Martin of
Tours, November 11)   131 **halcyon's days** peaceful times (the an-
cients believed that the bird called the halcyon nested on the sea
and that the waters remained calm during its breeding season)
138 **insulting** insolently triumphant   139 **bare** bore   141 **eagle** i.e.,
like Saint John the Evangelist, with the highest source of inspiration   142 **Helen** Saint Helena, inspired by a vision to find the cross
of Jesus   143 **Saint Philip's daughters** (who had the gift of prophecy; see Acts 21:9)

Bright star of Venus, fall'n down on the earth,
145   How may I reverently worship thee enough?

Alençon. Leave off delays, and let us raise the siege.

Reignier. Woman, do what thou canst to save our
      honors;
   Drive them from Orleans and be immortalized.

Dauphin. Presently° we'll try. Come, let's away about
      it;
150   No prophet will I trust, if she prove false.   *Exeunt.*

[Scene 3. *London. Before the Tower.*]

Enter Gloucester, with his Servingmen [in blue coats°].

Gloucester. I am come to survey° the Tower this
      day:
   Since Henry's death, I fear, there is conveyance.°
   Where be these warders,° that they wait not here?
   Open the gates; 'tis Gloucester° that calls.

First Warder. [*Within*] Who's there that knocks so
5   imperiously?

Gloucester's First [*Serving*]*man.* It is the noble Duke
      of Gloucester.

Second Warder. [*Within*] Whoe'er he be, you may not
      be let in.

Gloucester's First [*Serving*]*man.* Villains, answer you
      so the Lord Protector?

---

149 **Presently** immediately 1.3.s.d. **blue coats** (blue clothing was
customary for servants) 1 **survey** inspect 2 **conveyance** under-
hand dealing 3 **warders** guards 4 **Gloucester** (trisyllabic here
and often, for metrical purposes, elsewhere in the play)

First Warder. [*Within*] The Lord protect him! so we
 answer him;
 We do no otherwise than we are willed.   10

Gloucester. Who willèd you? Or whose will stands
 but mine?
 There's none Protector of the realm but I.
 Break up the gates, I'll be your warrantize;°
 Shall I be flouted thus by dunghill grooms?°
   Gloucester's men rush at the Tower gates, and
    Woodville the Lieutenant speaks within.

Woodville. What noise is this? What traitors have
 we here?   15

Gloucester. Lieutenant, is it you whose voice I hear?
 Open the gates; here's Gloucester that would enter.

Woodville. Have patience, noble duke, I may not
 open;
 The Cardinal of Winchester forbids:
 From him I have express commandment°   20
 That thou nor none of thine shall be let in.

Gloucester. Faint-hearted Woodville, prizest him 'fore
 me?°
 Arrogant Winchester, that haughty prelate,
 Whom Henry, our late sovereign, ne'er could
 brook?°
 Thou art no friend to God or to the king;   25
 Open the gates, or I'll shut thee out shortly.

Servingmen. Open the gates unto the Lord Protector,
 Or we'll burst them open, if that° you come not
 quickly.

 Enter to the Protector at the Tower gates Winchester
   and his men in tawny coats.°

---

13 **warrantize** pledge of security 14 **dunghill grooms** vile servingmen 20 **commandment** (trisyllabic; spelled *commandement* in the
Folio) 22 **prizest him 'fore me** rank him above me 24 **brook**
endure 28 **if that** if 28s.d. **tawny coats** (servants of churchmen
traditionally wore tawny, or brownish-yellow, coats)

Winchester. How now, ambitious Humphrey, what
 means this?

Gloucester. Peeled° priest, dost thou command me to
30 be shut out?

Winchester. I do, thou most usurping proditor,°
 And not Protector, of the king or realm.

Gloucester. Stand back, thou manifest conspirator,
 Thou that contriv'dst to murder our dead lord,
35 Thou that giv'st whores indulgences° to sin;
 I'll canvas thee in thy broad cardinal's hat,°
 If thou proceed in this thy insolence.

Winchester. Nay, stand thou back, I will not budge
 a foot;
 This be Damascus,° be thou cursèd Cain,
40 To slay thy brother° Abel, if thou wilt.

Gloucester. I will not slay thee, but I'll drive thee
 back;
 Thy scarlet robes as a child's bearing-cloth°
 I'll use to carry thee out of this place.

Winchester. Do what thou dar'st, I beard° thee to
 thy face.

Gloucester. What! am I dared and bearded to my
45 face?
 Draw, men, for all this privilegèd place,°
 Blue coats to tawny coats. Priest, beware your
 beard;
 I mean to tug it, and to cuff you soundly.
 Under my feet I stamp thy cardinal's hat;

---

30 **Peeled** tonsured, bald   31 **proditor** traitor   35 **indulgences** (the
brothels near the theaters on the south bank of the Thames were
within the jurisdiction of the Bishops of Winchester)   36 **canvas
. . . hat** toss you in your wide-brimmed ecclesiastical hat as if it were
a blanket   39 **Damascus** (supposed to have been built in the place
where Cain killed Abel)   40 **brother** (Winchester was half-brother
to Gloucester's father, King Henry IV)   42 **bearing-cloth** christen-
ing robe   44 **beard** defy   46 **for . . . place** (even though drawing
of weapons is forbidden under pain of death in royal residences)

In spite of pope or dignities of church,°　　50
　Here by the cheeks I'll drag thee up and down.

Winchester. Gloucester, thou wilt answer this before
　the pope.

Gloucester. Winchester goose,° I cry, a rope!° a rope!
　Now beat them hence; why do you let them stay?
　Thee I'll chase hence, thou wolf in sheep's array.　　55
　Out, tawny coats! out, scarlet° hypocrite!

*Here Gloucester's men beat out the Cardinal's men,
and enter in the hurly-burly° the Mayor of London
and his Officers.*

Mayor. Fie, lords! that you, being supreme
　magistrates,°
　Thus contumeliously° should break the peace!

Gloucester. Peace, mayor! thou know'st little of my
　wrongs:
　Here's Beaufort, that regards nor God nor king,　　60
　Hath here distrained° the Tower to his use.

Winchester. Here's Gloucester, a foe to citizens,
　One that still motions° war and never peace,
　O'ercharging your free purses with large fines,°
　That seeks to overthrow religion　　65
　Because he is Protector of the realm,
　And would have armor here out of the Tower
　To crown himself king and suppress° the prince.

Gloucester. I will not answer thee with words,
　but blows.　　　　　*Here they skirmish again.*

Mayor. Nought rests for me in this tumultuous strife　　70
　But to make open proclamation.

50 **dignities of church** your high ecclesiastical rank　53 **Winchester goose** (1) venereal infection (2) prostitute (see note to line 35)　53 **rope** hangman's cord　56 **scarlet** (a derisive allusion to the red robes of the cardinal)　56.s.d. **hurly-burly** tumult　57 **magistrates** administrators of the kingdom　58 **contumeliously** insolently　61 **distrained** seized　63 **still motions** always proposes　64 **O'ercharging . . . fines** overburdening you with excessive special taxes 68 **suppress** depose

    Come, officer, as loud as e'er thou canst,
    Cry.

    [*Officer.*] All manner of men assembled here in arms
75   this day against God's peace and the king's, we
    charge and command you, in his highness' name,
    to repair° to your several° dwelling-places; and not
    to wear, handle, or use any sword, weapon, or
    dagger henceforward, upon pain° of death.

80 *Gloucester.* Cardinal, I'll be no breaker of the law,
    But we shall meet, and break our minds at large.°

    Winchester. Gloucester, we'll meet to thy cost, be
    sure:
    Thy heart-blood I will have for this day's work.

    Mayor. I'll call for clubs,° if you will not away.
85   This cardinal's more haughty than the devil.

    Gloucester. Mayor, farewell; thou dost but what thou
    mayst.

    Winchester. Abominable Gloucester, guard thy head,
    For I intend to have it ere long.   *Exeunt.*

    Mayor. See the coast cleared, and then we will depart.
    Good God, these nobles should such stomachs
90   bear!°
    I myself fight not once in forty year.   *Exeunt.*

---

77 **repair** return 77 **several** own 79 **pain** penalty 81 **break . . .
large** reveal our thoughts fully 84 **call for clubs** i.e., summon the
apprentices of the city to come with clubs and assist the officers in
putting down the riot 90 **these . . . bear** that these noblemen
should have such quarrelsome tempers

[Scene 4. *Orleans.*]

Enter the Master Gunner of Orleans and his Boy.

Master Gunner. Sirrah,° thou know'st how Orleans is
besieged,
And how the English have the suburbs won.

Boy. Father, I know, and oft have shot at them,
Howe'er, unfortunate, I missed my aim.

Master Gunner. But now thou shalt not. Be thou ruled
by me: 5
Chief master-gunner am I of this town;
Something I must do to procure me grace.°
The prince's espials° have informèd me
How the English, in the suburbs close intrenched,
Went through a secret grate of iron bars   10
In yonder tower to overpeer° the city
And thence discover how with most advantage
They may vex us with shot or with assault.
To intercept° this inconvenience,
A piece of ordnance° 'gainst it I have placed,   15
And even these three days have I watched
If I could see them. Now do thou watch,
For I can stay no longer.
If thou spy'st any, run and bring me word,
And thou shalt find me at the governor's.   *Exit.* 20

Boy. Father, I warrant you, take you no care;
I'll never trouble you, if I may spy them.   *Exit.*

Enter Salisbury and Talbot on the turrets, with [*Sir
William Glansdale, Sir Thomas Gargrave, and*] *others.*

1.4.1 **Sirrah** a term used in addressing children or inferiors   7
grace favor   8 **espials** spies   11 **overpeer** look down upon   14
intercept stop   15 **piece of ordnance** cannon

Salisbury. Talbot, my life, my joy, again returned!
       How wert thou handled, being prisoner?
25   Or by what means gots thou° to be released?
       Discourse,° I prithee,° on this turret's top.

Talbot. The Earl of Bedford had a prisoner
       Called the brave Lord Ponton de Santrailles;
       For him was I exchanged and ransomèd.
30   But with a baser° man of arms by far
       Once in contempt they would have bartered me;
       Which I disdaining scorned and cravèd death
       Rather than I would be so pilled-esteemed.°
       In fine,° redeemed I was as I desired.
35   But O! the treacherous Falstaff wounds my heart,
       Whom with my bare fists I would execute,
       If I now had him brought into my power.

Salisbury. Yet tell'st thou not how thou wert enter-
       tained.

Talbot. With scoffs and scorns and contumelious
       taunts,
40   In open marketplace produced they me,
       To be a public spectacle to all:
       Here, said they, is the terror of the French,
       The scarecrow that affrights° our children so.
       Then broke I from the officers that led me,
45   And with my nails digged stones out of the ground
       To hurl at the beholders of my shame.
       My grisly° countenance made others fly;
       None durst come near for fear of sudden death.
       In iron walls they deemed me not secure;
50   So great fear of my name 'mongst them were spread
       That they supposed I could rend bars of steel
       And spurn in pieces posts of adamant.°
       Wherefore a guard of chosen shot° I had

---

25 **gots thou** did you manage   26 **Discourse** relate   26 **prithee**
pray thee   30 **baser** less well born   33 **pilled-esteemed** poorly
valued   34 **In fine** finally   43 **affrights** frightens   47 **grisly** grim
52 **adamant** indestructible material   53 **chosen shot** picked marks-
men

That walked about me every minute while,°
And if I did but stir out of my bed,   55
Ready they were to shoot me to the heart.

Enter the Boy with a linstock.°

Salisbury. I grieve to hear what torments you endured,
But we will be revenged sufficiently.
Now it is supper-time in Orleans;
Here, through this grate, I count each one   60
And view the Frenchmen how they fortify;
Let us look in; the sight will much delight thee.
Sir Thomas Gargrave, and Sir William Glansdale,
Let me have your express° opinions
Where is best place to make our batt'ry° next.   65

Gargrave. I think at the north gate, for there stands
lords.

Glansdale. And I, here, at the bulwark° of the bridge.

Talbot. For aught I see, this city must be famished,
Or with light skirmishes enfeeblèd.°   *Here they
shoot, and Salisbury [and Gargrave] fall down.*

Salisbury. O Lord, have mercy on us, wretched
sinners!   70

Gargrave. O Lord, have mercy on me, woeful man!

Talbot. What chance is this that suddenly hath
crossed° us?
Speak, Salisbury; at least, if thou canst speak,
How far'st thou, mirror of° all martial men?
One of thy eyes and thy cheek's side struck off!   75
Accursèd tower! accursèd fatal hand°
That hath contrived this woful tragedy!
In thirteen battles Salisbury o'ercame;
Henry the Fifth he first trained to the wars;

---

54 **every minute while** incessantly 56s.d. **linstock** staff to hold the match for lighting a cannon 64 **express** precise 65 **make our batt'ry** direct our fire 67 **bulwark** fortification 69 **enfeeblèd** weakened 72 **crossed** thwarted 74 **mirror of** model for 76 **fatal hand** hand of fate

80 Whilst any trump° did sound, or drum struck up,
     His sword did ne'er leave striking in the field.
     Yet liv'st thou, Salisbury? Though thy speech doth
        fail,
     One eye thou hast, to look to heaven for grace.
     The sun with one eye vieweth all the world.
85 Heaven, be thou gracious to none alive
     If Salisbury wants° mercy at thy hands!
     Bear hence his body; I will help to bury it.
     Sir Thomas Gargrave, hast thou any life?
     Speak unto Talbot; nay, look up to him.
90 Salisbury, cheer thy spirit with this comfort:
     Thou shalt not die whiles°—
     He beckons with his hand and smiles on me,
     As who° should say, "When I am dead and gone,
     Remember to avenge me on the French."
95 Plantagenet,° I will; and like thee, [Nero,]
     Play on the lute, beholding the towns burn.
     Wretched shall France be only in° my name.

Here an alarum, and it thunders and lightens.

     What stir° is this? What tumult's in the heavens?
     Whence cometh this alarum, and the noise?

Enter a Messenger.

Messenger. My lord, my lord, the French have gath-
100   ered head:°
     The Dolphin, with one Joan la Pucelle joined,
     A holy prophetess new risen up,
     Is come with a great power to raise the siege.

Here Salisbury lifteth himself up and groans.

Talbot. Hear, hear how dying Salisbury doth groan!
105 It irks his heart he cannot be revenged.

---

80 **trump** trumpet 86 **wants** lacks 91 **whiles** until 93 **As who**
as if he 95 **Plantagenet** (though Salisbury's name was Thomas
Montacute, he was related to the royal family, which adopted the
name Plantagenet in the fifteenth century) 97 **only in** merely at
the sound of (?) 98 **stir** commotion 100 **gathered head** raised
forces

Frenchmen, I'll be a Salisbury to you.
Pucelle or pussel,° Dolphin or dogfish,
Your hearts I'll stamp out with my horse's heels,
And make a quagmire of your mingled brains.
Convey me° Salisbury into his tent,   110
And then we'll try what these dastard Frenchmen
    dare.

                              Alarum. Exeunt.

                    [Scene 5. *Orleans.*]

*Here an alarum again, and Talbot pursueth the
Dauphin, and driveth him. Then enter Joan la Pucelle, driving Englishmen before her [and exit after
them]. Then [re-]enter Talbot.*

Talbot. Where is my strength, my valor, and my
    force?
  Our English troops retire, I cannot stay them;
  A woman clad in armor chaseth them.

                  Enter [La] Pucelle.

  Here, here she comes. I'll have a bout with thee;
  Devil or devil's dam,° I'll conjure thee:°   5
  Blood will I draw on thee,° thou art a witch,
  And straightway give thy soul to him thou serv'st.

Pucelle. Come, come, 'tis only° I that must disgrace
    thee.   *Here they fight.*

Talbot. Heavens, can you suffer hell so to prevail?
  My breast I'll burst with straining of my courage   10

107 **pussel** lewd woman, strumpet   110 **Convey me** carry   1.5.5 **dam**
(1) mistress (2) mother   5 **conjure thee** i.e., back to hell whence
you came   6 **Blood . . . thee** (whoever could draw blood from a
witch was free of her power)   8 **only** with no other assistance

And from my shoulders crack my arms asunder,
But I will chastise this high-minded° strumpet.

They fight again.

Pucelle. Talbot, farewell; thy hour is not yet come;
I must go victual° Orleans forthwith.°

A short alarum. Then enter the town with soldiers.

15   O'ertake me if thou canst; I scorn thy strength.
Go, go, cheer up thy hungry-starvèd men;
Help Salisbury to make his testament;
This day is ours, as many more shall be.   *Exit.*

Talbot. My thoughts are whirlèd like a potter's wheel;
20   I know not where I am, nor what I do.
A witch, by fear, not force, like Hannibal,°
Drives back our troops and conquers as she lists;°
So bees with smoke and doves with noisome stench
Are from their hives and houses driven away.
25   They called us for our fierceness English dogs;
Now, like to whelps,° we crying run away.

A short alarum.

Hark, countrymen! either renew the fight,
Or tear the lions° out of England's coat;
Renounce your soil,° give sheep in lions' stead:
30   Sheep run not half so treacherous° from the wolf,
Or horse or oxen from the leopard,
As you fly from your oft-subduèd slaves.

Alarum. Here another skirmish.

It will not be. Retire into your trenches.
You all consented unto Salisbury's death,
35   For none would strike a stroke in his revenge.
Pucelle is entered into Orleans
In spite of us or aught that we could do.

---

12 **high-minded** arrogant   14 **victual** bring provisions into   14 **forth-with** immediately   21 **Hannibal** (who terrified the Romans by driv-ing among them oxen with lighted torches fixed to their horns)
22 **lists** pleases   26 **whelps** puppies   28 **lions** heraldic royal sym-bol of England   29 **soil** (possibly a misprint for *style*; the line ap-pears to mean: replace the lions in your royal coat of arms with sheep)   30 **treacherous** fearfully

O, would I were to die with Salisbury!
The shame hereof will make me hide my head.
                    Exit Talbot. Alarum. Retreat.°

[Scene 6. *Orleans.*]

*Flourish. Enter on the walls [La] Pucelle, Dauphin,
Reignier, Alençon, and Soldiers.*

Pucelle. Advance° our waving colors on the walls;
    Rescued is Orleans from the English.
    Thus Joan la Pucelle hath performed her word.

Dauphin. Divinest creature, Astraea's daughter,°
    How shall I honor thee for this success?   5
    Thy promises are like Adonis'° garden
    That one day bloomed and fruitful were the next.
    France, triumph in thy glorious prophetess!
    Recovered is the town of Orleans;
    More blessèd hap° did ne'er befall our state.   10

Reignier. Why ring not out the bells aloud throughout
        the town?
    Dolphin, command the citizens make bonfires
    And feast and banquet in the open streets
    To celebrate the joy that God hath given us.

Alençon. All France will be replete with mirth and joy   15
    When they shall hear how we have played the
        men.°

Dauphin. 'Tis Joan, not we, by whom the day is won;

39s.d. **Retreat** signal for withdrawal from battle   1.6.1 **Advance**
raise   4 **Astraea's daughter** daughter of the goddess of justice
(compare *Deborah*, 1.2.105)   6 **Adonis'** of the youth loved by
Venus (for a description of his garden, see Edmund Spenser,
Faerie Queene, 3.6.29–50)   10 **hap** good fortune   16 **played the
men** proved our courage

For which I will divide my crown with her,
And all the priests and friars in my realm
20 Shall in procession sing her endless praise.
A statelier pyramis° to her I'll rear
Than Rhodope's° or Memphis' ever was.
In memory of her when she is dead,
Her ashes, in an urn more precious
25 Than the rich-jeweled coffer of Darius,°
Transported shall be at high festivals
Before the kings and queens of France.
No longer on Saint Denis° will we cry,
But Joan la Pucelle shall be France's saint.
30 Come in, and let us banquet royally,
After this golden day of victory.   *Flourish. Exeunt.*

21 **pyramis** pyramid   22 **Rhodope's** (according to legend, the
famous Greek courtesan Rhodopis built the third pyramid)
25 **coffer of Darius** (the Persian monarch's jewel chest, said to
have been used by Alexander the Great to hold a copy of
Homer)   28 **Saint Denis** patron saint of France

ACT 2

Scene 1. [*Orleans.*]

*Enter a [French] Sergeant of a band, with two
Sentinels.*

Sergeant. Sirs, take your places and be vigilant;
  If any noise or soldier you perceive
  Near to the walls, by some apparent sign
  Let us have knowledge at the court of guard.°

Sentinel. Sergeant, you shall. Thus are poor servi-
  tors,°   [*Exit Sergeant.*]   5
  When others sleep upon their quiet beds,
  Constrained to watch in darkness, rain, and cold.

*Enter Talbot, Bedford, and Burgundy, [and forces,]
with scaling-ladders, their drums beating a dead
march.*

Talbot. Lord Regent, and redoubted° Burgundy,
  By whose approach° the regions of Artois,
  Wallon, and Picardy° are friends to us,   10

2.1.4 **court of guard** headquarters of the guard   5 **servitors** soldiers
8 **redoubted** distinguished   9 **approach** presence   9–10 **Artois,
Wallon, and Picardy** (provinces in northeastern France, parts of
which are now in Belgium)

This happy night the Frenchmen are secure,°
Having all day caroused and banqueted;
Embrace we° then this opportunity
As fitting best to quittance° their deceit
15   Contrived by art° and baleful° sorcery.

Bedford. Coward of France! how much he wrongs his
     fame,
     Despairing of his own arm's fortitude,
     To join with witches and the help of hell.

Burgundy. Traitors have never other company.
20   But what's that Pucelle whom they term so pure?

Talbot. A maid, they say.

Bedford.   A maid? And be so martial?

Burgundy. Pray God she prove not masculine° ere
     long,
     If underneath the standard of the French
     She carry armor as she hath begun.

Talbot. Well, let them practice° and converse with
25   spirits.
     God is our fortress, in whose conquering name
     Let us resolve to scale their flinty° bulwarks.

Bedford. Ascend, brave Talbot; we will follow thee.

Talbot. Not all together: better far, I guess,
30   That we do make our entrance several° ways;
     That, if it chance the one of us do fail,
     The other yet may rise against their force.

Bedford. Agreed; I'll to yond° corner.

Burgundy.   And I to this.

Talbot. And here will Talbot mount, or make his
     grave.

11 **secure** careless   13 **Embrace we** let us seize   14 **quittance** re-
pay   15 **art** (black) magic   15 **baleful** harmful   22 **prove not masculine** (1) does not turn out to be a man (?) (2) does not become
pregnant with a male child   25 **practice** conjure   27 **flinty** rugged
30 **several** by separate   33 **yond** yonder

Now, Salisbury, for thee, and for the right   *35*
Of English Henry, shall this night appear
How much in duty I am bound to both.

Sentinel. Arm! arm! the enemy doth make assault!
    [*The English, scaling the walls,*] cry "St. George!
                a Talbot!" [*and enter the town*].

*The French leap o'er the walls in their shirts. Enter
several ways Bastard, Alençon, Reignier, half ready,°
                and half unready.*

Alençon. How now, my lords! what, all unready so?

Bastard. Unready? Ay, and glad we 'scaped so well.   *40*

Reignier. 'Twas time, I trow,° to wake and leave our
        beds,
Hearing alarums at our chamber doors.

Alençon. Of all exploits since first I followed arms,
Ne'er heard I of a warlike enterprise
More venturous or desperate than this.   *45*

Bastard. I think this Talbot be a fiend of hell.

Reignier. If not of hell, the heavens, sure, favor him.

Alençon. Here cometh Charles; I marvel how he
        sped.°

        Enter Charles [the Dauphin] and Joan.

Bastard. Tut, holy Joan was his defensive guard.

Dauphin. Is this thy cunning,° thou deceitful dame?   *50*
Didst thou at first, to flatter us withal,°
Make us partakers of a little gain,
That now our loss might be ten times so much?

Pucelle. Wherefore is Charles impatient with his
        friend?
At all times will you have my power alike?   *55*
Sleeping or waking must I still° prevail,

38s.d. **ready** dressed 41 **trow** think 48 **marvel how he sped** wonder how he fared 50 **cunning** craftiness 51 **to flatter us withal**
in order to deceive us 56 **still** always

Or will you blame and lay the fault on me?
Improvident° soldiers! had your watch been good,
This sudden mischief never could have fall'n.

60 *Dauphin.* Duke ofAlençon, this was your default,°
That, being captain of the watch tonight,
Did look no better to that weighty charge.°

Alençon. Had all your quarters been as safely kept
As that whereof I had the government,°
65 We had not been thus shamefully surprised.

Bastard. Mine was secure.

Reignier.   And so was mine, my lord.

Dauphin. And, for myself, most part of all this night,
Within her quarter° and mine own precinct°
I was employed in passing to and fro,
70 About relieving of the sentinels.
Then how or which way should they first break in?

Pucelle. Question, my lords, no further of the case,
How or which way; 'tis sure they found some place
But weakly guarded, where the breach was made.
75 And now there rests no other shift° but this,
To gather our soldiers, scattered and dispersed,
And lay new platforms to endamage them.°

*Alarum. Enter an [English] Soldier, crying, "A Tal-
bot! a Talbot!" They fly, leaving their clothes behind.*

Soldier. I'll be so bold to take what they have left.
The cry of Talbot serves me for a sword,
80 For I have loaden me° with many spoils,
Using no other weapon but his name.   *Exit.*

---

58 **Improvident** unwary 60 **default** fault 62 **weighty charge** important responsibility 64 **government** command 68 **quarter** (1)
assigned area for defense (2) chamber 68 **precinct** area of command 75 **shift** expedient, stratagem 77 **lay . . . them** make new
plans to harm the English 80 **loaden me** burdened myself

[Scene 2. *Orleans. Within the town.*]

Enter Talbot, Bedford, Burgundy, [a Captain, and others].

Bedford. The day begins to break, and night is fled,
　　Whose pitchy° mantle over-veiled the earth.
　　Here sound retreat, and cease our hot pursuit.

　　　　　　　　　　　　　　　　　　　　Retreat.

Talbot. Bring forth the body of old Salisbury,
　　And here advance it° in the marketplace,　　　　　　　　5
　　The middle center of this cursèd town.
　　Now have I paid my vow unto his soul;
　　For every drop of blood was drawn from him
　　There hath at least five Frenchmen died tonight.
　　And that hereafter ages may behold　　　　　　　　　10
　　What ruin happened in revenge of him,
　　Within their chiefest temple° I'll erect
　　A tomb, wherein his corpse shall be interred;
　　Upon the which, that everyone may read,
　　Shall be engraved the sack° of Orleans,　　　　　　　15
　　The treacherous manner of his mournful death,
　　And what a terror he had been to France.
　　But, lords, in all our bloody massacre,
　　I muse° we met not with the Dolphin's grace,°
　　His new-come champion, virtuous Joan of Arc,　　　20
　　Nor any of his false confederates.°

Bedford. 'Tis thought, Lord Talbot, when the fight began,
　　Roused on the sudden from their drowsy beds,

2.2.2 **pitchy** dark　5 **advance it** raise it up　12 **chiefest temple** cathedral　15 **sack** plundering　19 **muse** wonder why　19 **the Dolphin's grace** i.e., his grace, the Dauphin　21 **confederates** companions

They did amongst the troops of armèd men
25   Leap o'er the walls for refuge in the field.

Burgundy. Myself, as far as I could well discern
For° smoke and dusky vapors of the night,
Am sure I scared the Dolphin and his trull,°
When arm in arm they both came swiftly running,
30   Like to a pair of loving turtle-doves
That could not live asunder day or night,
After that things are set in order here,
We'll follow them with all the power we have.

Enter a Messenger.

Messenger. All hail, my lords! Which of this princely
train°
35   Call ye the warlike Talbot, for his acts
So much applauded through the realm of France?

Talbot. Here is the° Talbot; who would speak with
him?

Messenger. The virtuous lady, Countess of Auvergne,
With modesty admiring thy renown,
40   By me entreats, great lord, thou wouldst vouchsafe°
To visit her poor castle where she lies,°
That she may boast she hath beheld the man
Whose glory fills the world with loud report.

Burgundy. Is it even so? Nay, then, I see our wars
45   Will turn unto a peaceful comic sport,
When ladies crave to be encountered° with.
You may not, my lord, despise her gentle suit.°

Talbot. Ne'er trust me then; for when a world of men
Could not prevail with all their oratory,
50   Yet hath a woman's kindness overruled;°

---

27 **For** because of   28 **trull** concubine, harlot   34 **princely train**
noble company   37 **the** (used with the surname to designate the
head of a family or clan)   40 **vouchsafe** condescend   41 **lies** re-
sides   46 **encountered** met (for an amatory interview)   47 **gentle
suit** mannerly request   50 **overruled** prevailed

And therefore tell her I return great thanks
And in submission° will attend on her.
Will not your honors bear me company?

Bedford. No, truly, 'tis more than manners will,°
And I have heard it said, unbidden° guests   55
Are often welcomest when they are gone.

Talbot. Well then, alone, since there's no remedy,
I mean to prove this lady's courtesy.°
Come hither, captain. (*Whispers*) You perceive my
mind?°

Captain. I do, my lord, and mean accordingly.   60

Exeunt.

[Scene 3. *Auvergne. The Countess' castle.*]

Enter Countess [and her Porter].

Countess. Porter, remember what I gave in charge,°
And when you have done so, bring the keys to me.

Porter. Madam, I will.   *Exit.*

Countess. The plot is laid; if all things fall out right,
I shall as famous be by this exploit   5
As Scythian Tomyris° by Cyrus' death.
Great is the rumor° of this dreadful knight,
And his achievements of no less account;
Fain° would mine eyes be witness with mine ears,
To give their censure° of these rare reports.   10

Enter Messenger and Talbot.

52 **in submission** deferentially   54 **will** require   55 **unbidden** un-
invited   58 **prove . . . courtesy** try out this lady's hospitality   59
perceive my mind understand my plan   2.3.1 **gave in charge** in-
structed you to do   6 **Tomyris** queen of a fierce Central Asian people who slew Cyrus the Great in battle   7 **rumor** reputation   9
Fain gladly   10 **censure** judgment

Messenger. Madam,
          According as your ladyship desired,
          By message craved,° so is Lord Talbot come.

Countess. And he is welcome. What! is this the man?

Messenger. Madam, it is.

15   *Countess.*   Is this the scourge of France?
          Is this the Talbot, so much feared abroad
          That with his name the mothers still° their babes?
          I see report is fabulous° and false.
          I thought I should have seen some Hercules,
20   A second Hector, for his grim aspect°
          And large proportion of his strong-knit° limbs.
          Alas, this is a child, a silly° dwarf!
          It cannot be this weak and writhled° shrimp
          Should strike such terror to his enemies.

25   *Talbot.* Madam, I have been bold to trouble you,
          But since your ladyship is not at leisure,
          I'll sort° some other time to visit you.

Countess. What means he now? Go ask him whither
          he goes.

Messenger. Stay, my Lord Talbot, for my lady craves
30   To know the cause of your abrupt departure.

Talbot. Marry,° for that° she's in a wrong belief,
          I go to certify° her Talbot's here.

                    Enter Porter with keys.

Countess. If thou be he, then art thou prisoner.

Talbot. Prisoner! to whom?

Countess.   To me, bloodthirsty lord;
35   And for that cause I trained° thee to my house.
          Long time thy shadow hath been thrall to me,

---

13 **craved** invited   17 **still** silence   18 **fabulous** merely fictional
20 **aspect** countenance   21 **strong-knit** well-muscled   22 **silly** feeble
23 **writhled** wrinkled   27 **sort** choose   31 **Marry** why   31 **for that**
because   32 **certify** inform   35 **trained** lured

For in my gallery thy picture° hangs.
But now the substance shall endure the like,
And I will chain these legs and arms of thine
That hast by tyranny these many years   40
Wasted our country, slain our citizens,
And sent our sons and husbands captive.°

Talbot. Ha, ha, ha!

Countess. Laughest thou, wretch? Thy mirth shall turn
    to moan.

Talbot. I laugh to see your ladyship so fond°   45
To think that you have aught but Talbot's shadow
Whereon to practice your severity.°

Countess. Why, art not thou the man?

Talbot.   I am indeed.

Countess. Then have I substance too.

Talbot. No, no, I am but shadow of myself: 50
You are deceived, my substance is not here,
For what you see is but the smallest part
And least proportion of humanity.
I tell you, madam, were the whole frame° here,
It is of such a spacious lofty pitch,°   55
Your roof were not sufficient to contain 't.

Countess. This· is a riddling merchant° for the
    nonce;°
He will be here, and yet he is not here.
How can these contrarieties° agree?

Talbot. That will I show you presently.   60
             Winds° his horn; drums strike up; a peal
                  of ordnance;° enter Soldiers.
How say you, madam? Are you now persuaded
That Talbot is but shadow of himself?

---

37 **picture** (possibly implying that the Countess was trying to practice witchcraft on him)   42 **captivate** captive   45 **fond** foolish   47
severity cruelty   54 **frame** structure   55 **pitch** stature   57 **riddling
merchant** enigmatic fellow   57 **for the nonce** for the occasion
(merely a line-filler)   59 **contrarieties** contradictions   60s.d **Winds**
blows   60s.d. **peal of ordnance** salute of guns

These are his substance, sinews, arms, and strength,
With which he yoketh° your rebellious necks,
65 Razeth your cities and subverts° your towns,
And in a moment makes them desolate.

Countess. Victorious Talbot, pardon my abuse;
I find thou art no less than fame hath bruited°
And more than may be gathered by thy shape.
70 Let my presumption not provoke thy wrath,
For I am sorry that with reverence°
I did not entertain thee as thou art.

Talbot. Be not dismayed, fair lady, nor misconster°
The mind of Talbot, as you did mistake
75 The outward composition° of his body.
What you have done hath not offended me,
Nor other satisfaction do I crave,
But only, with your patience, that we may
Taste of your wine and see what cates° you have,
80 For soldiers' stomachs always serve them well.

Countess. With all my heart, and think me honorèd
To feast so great a warrior in my house.   *Exeunt.*

[Scene 4. *London. The Temple Garden.*°]

Enter Richard Plantagenet, Warwick, Somerset, [*William de la*] *Pole* [*Earl of Suffolk, Vernon, and another Lawyer*].

Plantagenet. Great lords and gentlemen, what means
this silence?
Dare no man answer in a case of truth?

____

64 **yoketh** brings into subjection   65 **subverts** overthrows   68
bruited reported   71 **reverence** respect   73 **misconster** misunderstand   75 **composition** form   79 **cates** choice foods   2.4.s.d.
Temple Garden (the Inner and Middle Temples were residences for
students of the common law)

Suffolk. Within the Temple Hall we were too loud;
 The garden here is more convenient.

Plantagenet. Then say at once if I maintained the
  truth;   5
 Or else was wrangling° Somerset in th' error?

Suffolk. Faith,° I have been a truant° in the law,
 And never yet could frame° my will to it,
 And therefore frame° the law unto my will.

Somerset. Judge you, my lord of Warwick, then,
  between us.   10

Warwick. Between two hawks, which flies the higher
  pitch;
 Between two dogs, which hath the deeper mouth;°
 Between two blades, which bears the better temper;
 Between two horses, which doth bear him° best;
 Between two girls, which hath the merriest eye—   15
 I have perhaps some shallow spirit° of judgment;
 But in these nice sharp quillets° of the law,
 Good faith, I am no wiser than a daw.°

Plantagenet. Tut, tut, here is a mannerly forbearance.
 The truth appears so naked on my side   20
 That any purblind° eye may find it out.

Somerset. And on my side it is so well appareled,°
 So clear, so shining, and so evident,
 That it will glimmer through a blind man's eye.

Plantagenet. Since you are tongue-tied and so loath
  to speak,   25
 In dumb significants° proclaim your thoughts:
 Let him that is a true-born gentleman
 And stands upon° the honor of his birth,

---

6 **wrangling** quarrelsome   7 **Faith** in truth   7 **truant** lazy student
8 **frame** dispose   9 **frame** twist   12 **mouth** bark, bay   14 **bear him**
behave himself   16 **shallow spirit** small amount   17 **nice sharp
quillets** precise and subtle distinctions   18 **daw** simpleton   21
purblind nearly blind   22 **appareled** (1) dressed (2) ordered   26 **In
dumb significants** by mute signs   28 **stands upon** takes pride in

    If he suppose that I have pleaded truth,
30   From off this brier pluck a white rose with me.

Somerset. Let him that is no coward nor no flatterer,
    But dare maintain the party of the truth,
    Pluck a red rose from off this thorn with me.

Warwick. I love no colors;° and without all color
35   Of base insinuating flattery
    I pluck this white rose with Plantagenet.

Suffolk. I pluck this red rose with young Somerset
    And say withal° I think he held the right.

Vernon. Stay, lords and gentlemen, and pluck no more
40   Till you conclude that he upon whose side
    The fewest roses are cropped° from the tree
    Shall yield the other in the right opinion.

Somerset. Good Master Vernon, it is well objected;°
    If I have fewest, I subscribe in silence.

45 *Plantagenet.* And I.

Vernon. Then for the truth and plainness of the case,
    I pluck this pale and maiden° blossom here,
    Giving my verdict on the white rose side.

Somerset. Prick not your finger as you pluck it off,
50   Lest bleeding you do paint the white rose red
    And fall on my side so against your will.

Vernon. If I, my lord, for my opinion bleed,
    Opinion shall be surgeon to my hurt
    And keep me on the side where still I am.

55 *Somerset.* Well, well, come on, who else?

Lawyer. Unless my study and my books be false,
    The argument you held was wrong in you;
    In sign whereof I pluck a white rose too.

Plantagenet. Now, Somerset, where is your argument?

---

34 **colors** (1) pretenses (2) adornments of speech   38 **withal** thereby
41 **cropped** plucked   43 **objected** proposed   47 **maiden** flawless

Somerset. Here in my scabbard, meditating° that   60
    Shall dye your white rose in a bloody red.

Plantagenet. Meantime your cheeks do counterfeit°
    our roses,
    For pale they look with fear, as witnessing
    The truth on our side.

Somerset.   No, Plantagenet,
    'Tis not for fear, but anger that thy cheeks   65
    Blush for pure shame to counterfeit our roses,
    And yet thy tongue will not confess thy error.

Plantagenet. Hath not thy rose a canker,° Somerset?

Somerset. Hath not thy rose a thorn, Plantagenet?

Plantagenet. Ay, sharp and piercing, to maintain his
    truth   70
    Whiles thy consuming canker eats his falsehood.

Somerset. Well, I'll find friends to wear my bleeding
    roses,
    That shall maintain what I have said is true
    Where false Plantagenet dare not be seen.

Plantagenet. Now, by this maiden blossom in my
    hand,   75
    I scorn thee and thy fashion,° peevish boy.

Suffolk. Turn not thy scorns this way, Plantagenet.

Plantagenet. Proud Pole, I will, and scorn both him
    and thee.

Suffolk. I'll turn my part thereof into thy throat.

Somerset. Away, away, good William de la Pole!   80
    We grace the yeoman° by conversing with him.

Warwick. Now, by God's will, thou wrong'st him,
    Somerset;

---

60 **meditating** planning   62 **counterfeit** imitate   68 **canker** (1) disease (2) caterpillar larva   76 **fashion** (1) manner of behavior (2) faction (?)   81 **grace the yeoman** dignify this commoner

His grandfather° was Lionel Duke of Clarence,
Third son to the third Edward King of England:
85   Spring crestless° yeomen from so deep a root?

Plantagenet. He bears him on the place's privilege,°
     Or durst not, for his craven heart, say thus.

Somerset. By him that made me, I'll maintain my
          words
     On any plot of ground in Christendom.
90   Was not thy father, Richard Earl of Cambridge,
     For treason executed in our late king's days?
     And, by his treason, stand'st not thou attainted,
     Corrupted, and exempt from ancient gentry?°
     His trespass° yet lives guilty in thy blood,
95   And, till thou be restored, thou art a yeoman.°

Plantagenet. My father was attachèd,° not attainted,
     Condemned to die for treason, but no traitor;
     And that I'll prove° on better men than Somerset,
     Were growing time once ripened to my will.°
100   For your partaker° Pole and you yourself,
     I'll note you in my book of memory
     To scourge you for this apprehension.°
     Look to it well and say you are well warned.

Somerset. Ah, thou shalt find us ready for thee still,
105   And know us by these colors for thy foes,
     For these my friends in spite of thee shall wear.

Plantagenet. And, by my soul, this pale and angry
          rose,
     As cognizance° of my blood-drinking° hate,

---

83 **grandfather** i.e., great-great-grandfather 85 **crestless** not having the right to a coat of arms 86 **privilege** i.e., of sanctuary (since
the Temple was founded as a religious house) 92–93 **attainted . . .
gentry** (legal penalties by which the heirs of a person convicted of
treason were prevented from inheriting his property and titles) 94
trespass crime 95 **And . . . yeoman** (therefore, you shall remain a
commoner until your titles are legally restored) 96 **attachèd** ar-
rested 98 **prove** establish through trial by combat 99 **Were . . .
will** i.e., if I should ever be restored to the nobility 100 **partaker**
partisan 102 **apprehension** notion, display of wit 108 **cognizance**
a badge 108 **blood-drinking** bloodthirsty

Will I forever and my faction wear
Until it wither with me to my grave   110
Or flourish to the height of my degree.°

Suffolk. Go forward and be choked with thy ambition!
   And so farewell until I meet thee next.   *Exit.*

Somerset. Have with thee,° Pole. Farewell, ambitious Richard.   *Exit.*

Plantagenet. How I am braved° and must perforce°
   endure it!   115

Warwick. This blot that they object against your house
   Shall be whipped° out in the next parliament
   Called for the truce of Winchester and Gloucester,
   And if thou be not then created York,°
   I will not live to be accounted° Warwick.   120
   Meantime, in signal of my love to thee,
   Against proud Somerset and William Pole,
   Will I upon thy party° wear this rose.
   And here I prophesy: this brawl° today,
   Grown to this faction in the Temple Garden,   ·125
   Shall send, between the red rose and the white,
   A thousand souls to death and deadly night.

Plantagenet. Good Master Vernon, I am bound to
   you
   That you on my behalf would pluck a flower.

Vernon. In your behalf still will I wear the same.   130

Lawyer. And so will I.

Plantagenet. Thanks, gentle [sir].
   Come, let us four to dinner: I dare say
   This quarrel will drink blood° another day.   *Exeunt.*

---

111 **to . . . degree** until I regain my high rank   114 **Have with thee**
I'll go with you   115 **braved** defied   115 **perforce** necessarily
117 **whipped** quickly stricken   119 **York** i.e., Duke of York   120
accounted considered   123 **upon thy party** in support of you   124
brawl quarrel   134 **drink blood** result in bloodshed

[Scene 5. *The Tower of London.*]

Enter Mortimer, brought in a chair, and Jailers.

Mortimer. Kind keepers of my weak decaying age,
　　Let dying Mortimer here rest himself.
　　Even like a man new halèd from the rack,°
　　So fare my limbs with long imprisonment,
5　　And these gray locks, the pursuivants° of death,
　　Nestor-like° agèd in an age of care,
　　Argue° the end of Edmund Mortimer.
　　These eyes, like lamps whose wasting° oil is spent,
　　Wax° dim, as drawing to their exigent;°
10　　Weak shoulders, overborne with burthening° grief,
　　And pithless° arms, like to a withered vine
　　That droops his sapless branches to the ground.
　　Yet are these feet, whose strengthless stay° is numb,
　　Unable to support this lump of clay,
15　　Swift-wingèd with desire to get a grave,
　　As witting I no other comfort have.
　　But tell me, keeper, will my nephew come?

First Jailer. Richard Plantagenet, my lord, will come:
　　We sent unto the Temple, unto his chamber,
20　　And answer was returned that he will come.

Mortimer. Enough; my soul shall then be satisfied.
　　Poor gentleman! his wrong doth equal mine.
　　Since Henry Monmouth° first began to reign,
　　Before whose glory I was great in arms,

2.5.3 **new . . . rack** just released from the torturer's rack　5 **pursuivants** heralds　6 **Nestor-like** (the Greek king Nestor, in Homer's *Iliad,* is a type of old age)　7 **Argue** foretell　8 **wasting** consuming　9 **Wax** grow　9 **exigent** end　10 **burthening** (dissyllabic) burdensome　11 **pithless** strengthless　13 **stay** support　23 **Henry Monmouth** King Henry V

This loathsome sequestration° have I had;   25
And even since then hath Richard been obscured,°
Deprived of honor and inheritance.
But now the arbitrator of despairs,
Just Death, kind umpire° of men's miseries,
With sweet enlargement° doth dismiss me hence.   30
I would his° troubles likewise were expired,
That so he might recover what was lost.

Enter Richard [Plantagenet].

First Jailer. My lord, your loving nephew now is
    come.

Mortimer. Richard Plantagenet, my friend, is he
    come?

Plantagenet. Ay, noble uncle, thus ignobly used,   35
    Your nephew, late despisèd° Richard, comes.

Mortimer. Direct mine arms I may° embrace his neck
    And in his bosom spend my latter gasp.°
    O, tell me when my lips do touch his cheeks,
    That I may kindly give one fainting kiss.   40
    And now declare, sweet stem from York's great
        stock,°
    Why didst thou say, of late thou wert despised?

Plantagenet. First, lean thine agèd back against mine
        arm,
    And, in that ease, I'll tell thee my disease.°
    This day, in argument upon a case,   45
    Some words there grew 'twixt Somerset and me;
    Among which terms he used his lavish° tongue
    And did upbraid° me with my father's death:
    Which obloquy° set bars before my tongue,
    Else with the like I had requited° him.   50

25 **sequestration** imprisonment 26 **obscured** degraded 29 **umpire** arbitrator 30 **enlargement** release 31 **his** i.e., Plantagenet's 36 **late despisèd** just insulted 37 **I may** (so that) I may 38 **spend my latter gasp** draw my last breath 41 **stock** trunk (i.e., lineage) 44 **disease** source of my discomfort 47 **lavish** licentious, unrestrained 48 **upbraid** insult 49 **obloquy** reproach 50 **requited** repaid

Therefore, good uncle, for my father's sake,
In honor of a true Plantagenet,
And for alliance' sake, declare the cause°
My father, Earl of Cambridge, lost his head.

Mortimer. That cause, fair nephew, that imprisoned
55   me
And hath detained me all my flow'ring° youth
Within a loathsome dungeon, there to pine,
Was cursèd instrument of his decease.

Plantagenet. Discover° more at large what cause that
     was,
60   For I am ignorant and cannot guess.

Mortimer. I will, if that my fading breath permit
And death approach not ere my tale be done.
Henry the Fourth, grandfather to this king,
Deposed his nephew° Richard, Edward's son,
65   The first-begotten and the lawful heir
Of Edward king, the third of that descent:°
During whose reign the Percies° of the north,
Finding his usurpation most unjust,
Endeavored my advancement to the throne.
70   The reason moved° these warlike lords to this
Was, for that—young° Richard thus removed,
Leaving no heir begotten of his body—
I was the next by birth and parentage:
For by my mother° I derivèd° am
75   From Lionel Duke of Clarence, third son
To King Edward the Third; whereas he
From John of Gaunt doth bring his pedigree,
Being but fourth of that heroic line.
But mark:° as in this haughty° great attempt

53 **the cause** for what reason   56 **flow'ring** vigorous, flourishing
59 **Discover** explain   64 **nephew** (cousin)   64–66 **Edward's . . .
descent** i.e., Richard II, son of Edward the Black Prince and grand-
son of King Edward III   67 **Percies** noble family of Northumberland   70 **moved** that provoked   71 **young** (Richard was actually
over thirty at the time of his deposition)   74 **mother** (actually,
grandmother)   74 **derivèd** descended   79 **mark** listen attentively
79 **haughty** lofty

They labored to plant the rightful heir,   80
I lost my liberty and they their lives.
Long after this, when Henry the Fifth,
Succeeding his father Bolingbroke, did reign,
Thy father, Earl of Cambridge, then derived
From famous Edmund Langley, Duke of York,   85
Marrying my sister that thy mother was,
Again, in pity of my hard distress,
Levied an army, weening to redeem
And have installed me in the diadem;°
But, as the rest, so fell that noble earl   90
And was beheaded. Thus the Mortimers,
In whom the title rested, were suppressed.

Plantagenet. Of which, my lord, your honor is the
    last.

Mortimer. True; and thou seest that I no issue have
And that my fainting words do warrant° death.   95
Thou art my heir; the rest I wish thee gather,°
But yet be wary in thy studious care.°

Plantagenet. Thy grave admonishments prevail with
    me,
But yet, methinks, my father's execution
Was nothing less than bloody tyranny.   100

Mortimer. With silence, nephew, be thou politic:
Strong-fixèd is the house of Lancaster,
And like a mountain, not to be removed.
But now thy uncle is removing hence,
As princes do their courts, when they are cloyed°   105
With long continuance in a settled place.

Plantagenet. O, uncle, would some part of my young
    years

88–89 **Levied . . . diadem** raised an army, with the intention of
rescuing me and having me crowned king   95 **warrant** give assur-
ance of   96 **the rest . . . gather** (1) I want you to conclude for yourself (2) I hope that you may gain all that is rightfully yours   97
But . . . care i.e., but always be careful even as you take pains in
this enterprise   105 **cloyed** satiated

Might but redeem the passage° of your age!

Mortimer. Thou dost then wrong me, as that
    slaughterer doth
110 Which giveth many wounds when one will kill.
Mourn not, except thou sorrow for my good;
Only give order° for my funeral.
And so farewell, and fair be all thy hopes,
And prosperous be thy life in peace and war! *Dies.*

Plantagenet. And peace, no war, befall thy parting
115 soul!
In prison hast thou spent a pilgrimage°
And like a hermit overpassed° thy days.
Well, I will lock his counsel in my breast,
And what I do imagine, let that rest.
120 Keepers, convey him hence, and I myself
Will see his burial better than his life.°

    [*Exeunt Jailers with the body of Mortimer.*]

Here dies the dusky° torch of Mortimer,
Choked with ambition of the meaner sort.°
And for those wrongs, those bitter injuries
125 Which Somerset hath offered to my house,
I doubt not but with honor to redress.°
And therefore haste I to the parliament,
Either to be restorèd to my blood,
Or make my will th'advantage of my good.°

                       Exit.

---

108 **redeem the passage** buy back the passing 112 **give order** make
arrangements 116 **pilgrimage** full life's journey 117 **overpassed**
lived out 121 **Will . . . life** will see that he receives the honor in
his funeral that was denied him during his lifetime 122 **dusky**
gloomy 123 **Choked . . . sort** stifled by the ambition of men of
inferior birth (i.e., the House of Lancaster) 126 **redress** remedy
129 **will . . . good** determination of purpose the means of achieving
my ambition (see Textual Note)

ACT 3

Scene 1. [*London. The Parliament-house.*]

Flourish. Enter King, Exeter, Gloucester, Win-
chester, Warwick, Somerset, Suffolk, Richard
Plantagenet. Gloucester offers to put up a bill;°
Winchester snatches it, tears it.

Winchester. Com'st thou with deep premeditated
    lines,°
With written pamphlets studiously devised?
Humphrey of Gloucester, if thou canst accuse
Or aught intend'st to lay unto my charge,
Do it without invention,° suddenly,   5
As I with sudden and extemporal° speech
Purpose to answer what thou canst object.

Gloucester. Presumptuous priest! this place commands
    my patience,
Or thou shouldst find thou hast dishonored me.
Think not, although in writing I preferred°   10
The manner of thy vile outrageous crimes,

3.1.s.d. **offers . . . bill** attempts to post a statement of accusations
1 **deep premeditated lines** statements carefully thought out in advance 5 **invention** (seeking out the grounds for argument in the
manner of a rhetorician or a lawyer trained in oratory) 6 **ex-**
temporal extemporaneous 10 **preferred** set forth

69

That therefore I have forged,° or am not able
Verbatim to rehearse the method of my pen.°
No, prelate, such is thy audacious wickedness,
15   Thy lewd, pestiferous, and dissentious pranks,°
As very° infants prattle of thy pride.
Thou art a most pernicious usurer,°
Froward° by nature, enemy to peace,
Lascivious, wanton, more than well beseems°
20   A man of thy profession and degree.
And for thy treachery, what's more manifest?
In that thou laid'st a trap to take my life,
As well at London Bridge as at the Tower.
Beside, I fear me, if thy thoughts were sifted,°
25   The king, thy sovereign, is not quite exempt
From envious malice of thy swelling° heart.

Winchester. Gloucester, I do defy thee. Lords, vouchsafe
    To give me hearing what I shall reply.
    If I were covetous, ambitious, or perverse,
30   As he will have me,° how am I so poor?
Or how haps it° I seek not to advance
Or raise myself, but keep my wonted calling?°
And for dissension, who preferreth peace
More than I do?—except I be provoked.
35   No, my good lords, it is not that offends;
It is not that that hath incensed° the duke:
It is, because no one should sway° but he,
No one but he should be about the king,
And that engenders thunder in his breast
40   And makes him roar these accusations forth.
But he shall know I am as good—

---

12 **forged** fabricated lies   13 **rehearse . . . pen** repeat the contents
of what I have written   15 **lewd . . . pranks** wicked, mischievous,
and quarrelsome offenses   16 **As very** that even   17 **pernicious
usurer** (alluding to Winchester's reputation for gaining riches
through extortions and loans made at exorbitant rates of interest)
18 **Froward** inclined to evil   19 **beseems** is fitting to   24 **sifted**
closely examined   26 **swelling** proud   30 **have me** make me out to
be   31 **haps it** does it happen   32 **calling** religious vocation   36
incensed enraged   37 **sway** rule

Gloucester.   As good?
  Thou bastard° of my grandfather!

Winchester. Ay, lordly° sir; for what are you, I pray,
  But one imperious° in another's throne?

Gloucester. Am I not Protector, saucy priest?   45

Winchester. And am not I a prelate of the church?

Gloucester. Yes, as an outlaw in a castle keeps
  And useth it to patronage° his theft.

Winchester. Unreverent Gloucester!

Gloucester.   Thou art reverent
  Touching thy spiritual function,° not thy life.   50

Winchester. Rome shall remedy this.

Warwick.   Roam thither, then.
  My lord, it were your duty to forbear.

Somerset. Ay, see the bishop be not overborne.°
  Methinks my lord° should be religious
  And know the office° that belongs to such.   55

Warwick. Methinks his lordship° should be humbler;
  It fitteth not a prelate so to plead.

Somerset. Yes, when his holy state is touched so
    near.°

Warwick. State holy or unhallowed,° what of that?
  Is not his grace° Protector to the king?   60

Plantagenet. [*Aside*] Plantagenet, I see, must hold
    his tongue,
  Lest it be said, "Speak, sirrah, when you should;

42 **bastard** (Winchester was an illegitimate son of John of Gaunt,
Duke of Lancaster) 43 **lordly** haughty 44 **imperious** ruling 48
patronage defend 50 **Touching . . . function** only in respect of
your high ecclesiastical office 53 **overborne** prevailed over 54
lord i.e., Gloucester 55 **office** respect 56 **lordship** Winchester
58 **holy . . . near** ecclesiastical office is so directly involved 59
holy or unhallowed ecclesiastical or secular 60 **grace** i.e.,
Gloucester

Must your bold verdict° enter talk with lords?"
Else would I have a fling at° Winchester.

65 *King.* Uncles of Gloucester and of Winchester,
The special watchmen° of our English weal,°
I would prevail, if prayers might prevail,
To join your hearts in love and amity.
O, what a scandal is it to our crown,
70 That two such noble peers as ye should jar!
Believe me, lords, my tender years can tell
Civil dissension is a viperous worm°
That gnaws the bowels of the commonwealth.

A noise within, "Down with the tawny-coats!"

What tumult's this?

Warwick.   An uproar, I dare warrant,°
75 Begun through malice of the bishop's men.

A noise again, "Stones! stones!"

Enter Mayor.

Mayor. O my good lords, and virtuous Henry,
Pity the city of London, pity us!
The bishop° and the Duke of Gloucester's men,
Forbidden late° to carry any weapon,
80 Have filled their pockets full of pebble stones
And banding themselves in contrary parts°
Do pelt so fast at one another's pate°
That many have their giddy° brains knocked out.
Our windows are broke down in every street,
85 And we for fear compelled to shut our shops.

*Enter [Servingmen of Gloucester and Winchester]
in skirmish, with bloody pates.*

King. We charge you, on allegiance to ourself,
To hold your slaught'ring hands and keep the
peace.

63 **bold verdict** presumptuous opinion 64 **have a fling at** reprove
66 **watchmen** guardians 66 **weal** state 72 **worm** serpent 74 **warrant** swear 78 **bishop** bishop's 79 **late** recently 81 **parts** parties
82 **pate** head 83 **giddy** foolish

Pray, uncle Gloucester, mitigate° this strife.

First Servingman. Nay, if we be forbidden stones,
  we'll fall to it with our teeth.   90

Second Servingman. Do what ye dare, we are as
  resolute.   *Skirmish again.*

Gloucester. You of my household, leave this peevish
    broil
  And set this unaccustomed° fight aside.

Third Servingman. My lord, we know your grace to be
    a man   95
  Just and upright; and, for your royal birth,
  Inferior to none but to his majesty,
  And ere that we will suffer° such a prince,
  So kind a father of the commonweal,
  To be disgracèd by an inkhorn mate,°   100
  We and our wives and children all will fight
  And have our bodies slaughtered by thy foes.

First Servingman. Ay, and the very parings of our
    nails
  Shall pitch a field° when we are dead. *Begin again.*

Gloucester.   Stay, stay, I say!
  And if you love me, as you say you do,   105
  Let me persuade you to forbear awhile.

King. O, how this discord doth afflict my soul!
  Can you, my Lord of Winchester, behold
  My sighs and tears and will not once relent?
  Who should be pitiful, if you be not?   110
  Or who should study° to prefer a peace,
  If holy churchmen take delight in broils?

Warwick. Yield, my Lord Protector; yield, Winchester,

---

88 **mitigate** appease   94 **unaccustomed** indecorous   98 **suffer** permit   100 **inkhorn mate** scribbling fellow (an unlettered person's
disparaging allusion to the literacy of clergymen)   104 **pitch a
field** i.e., serve as stakes in a pitched battlefield   111 **study** make
it his aim

Except° you mean with obstinate repulse°
115   To slay your sovereign and destroy the realm.
You see what mischief and what murder too
Hath been enacted through your enmity;
Then be at peace, except ye thirst for blood.

Winchester. He shall submit, or I will never yield.

Gloucester. Compassion on the king commands me
120   stoop;
Or I would see his heart out ere the priest
Should ever get that privilege° of me.

Warwick. Behold, my Lord of Winchester, the duke
Hath banished moody discontented fury,
125   As by his smoothèd brows it doth appear:
Why look you still so stern and tragical?°

Gloucester. Here, Winchester, I offer thee my hand.

King. Fie, uncle Beaufort! I have heard you preach
That malice was a great and grievous sin,
130   And will not you maintain the thing you teach,
But prove a chief offender in the same?

Warwick. Sweet king! the bishop hath a kindly gird.°
For shame, my Lord of Winchester, relent!
What, shall a child instruct you what to do?

Winchester. Well, Duke of Gloucester, I will yield
135   to thee
Love for thy love, and hand for hand I give.

Gloucester. [*Aside*] Ay, but, I fear me, with a hollow°
heart.
[*Aloud*] See here, my friends and loving countrymen;
This token° serveth for a flag of truce
140   Betwixt ourselves and all our followers.
So help me God, as I dissemble not!

---

114 **Except** unless   114 **repulse** refusal   122 **privilege** advantage
yielded   126 **tragical** gloomy   132 **kindly gird** fitting gibe   137
hollow insincere   139 **token** i.e., handclasp

Winchester. [*Aside*] So help me God, as I intend it
   not!

King. O loving uncle, kind Duke of Gloucester,
   How joyful am I made by this contract!°
   Away, my masters! trouble us no more,   *145*
   But join in friendship, as your lords have done.

First Servingman. Content; I'll to the surgeon's.

Second Servingman.   And so will I.

Third Servingman. And I will see what physic° the
   tavern affords.°   *Exeunt.*

Warwick. Accept this scroll,° most gracious sovereign,   *150*
   Which in the right of Richard Plantagenet
   We do exhibit to your majesty.

Gloucester. Well urged, my Lord of Warwick: for,
   sweet prince,
   And if° your grace mark° every circumstance,
   You have great reason to do Richard right,   *155*
   Especially for those occasions°
   At Eltham Place I told your majesty.

King. And those occasions, uncle, were of force.
   Therefore, my loving lords, our pleasure is
   That Richard be restorèd to his blood.°   *160*

Warwick. Let Richard be restorèd to his blood;
   So shall his father's wrongs be recompensed.

Winchester. As will the rest, so willeth Winchester.

King. If Richard will be true, not that all alone
   But all the whole inheritance I give   *165*
   That doth belong unto the house of York,
   From whence you spring by lineal descent.

Plantagenet. Thy humble servant vows obedience
   And humble service till the point of death.

144 **contract** agreement   148 **physic** remedy   149 **affords** provides
150 **scroll** document   154 **And if** if   154 **mark** take notice of   156
occasions reasons   160 **blood** i.e., title and rights of nobility

170 *King.* Stoop then and set your knee against my foot,
      And in reguerdon° of that duty done,
      I girt° thee with the valiant sword of York.
      Rise, Richard, like a true Plantagenet,
      And rise created princely Duke of York.

Plantagenet. And so thrive Richard as thy foes may
175   fall!
      And as my duty springs, so perish they
      That grudge one thought° against your majesty!

All. Welcome, high prince, the mighty Duke of York!

Somerset. [*Aside*] Perish, base prince, ignoble Duke
      of York!

180 *Gloucester.* Now will it best avail your majesty
      To cross the seas and to be crowned in France:
      The presence of a king engenders love
      Amongst his subjects and his loyal friends,
      As it disanimates° his enemies.

King. When Gloucester says the word, King Henry
185   goes,
      For friendly counsel cuts off many foes.

Gloucester. Your ships already are in readiness.

            Sennet.° Flourish. Exeunt. Manet° Exeter.

Exeter. Ay, we may march in England or in France,
      Not seeing what is likely to ensue.
190 This late dissension grown betwixt the peers
      Burns under feignèd ashes of forged° love
      And will at last break out into a flame;
      As festered members° rot but by degree°
      Till bones and flesh and sinews fall away,
195 So will this base and envious discord breed.
      And now I fear that fatal prophecy

171 **reguerdon** ample reward   172 **girt** gird   177 **grudge one
thought** entertain one grudging thought   184 **disanimates** disheart-
ens   187s.d. **Sennet** trumpet signal for the exit of an important
personage   187s.d. **Manet** remains (Latin)   191 **forged** pretended
193 **members** parts of the body   193 **by degree** little by little,
gradually

Which in the time of Henry named the Fifth
Was in the mouth of every sucking° babe,
That Henry born at Monmouth should win all
And Henry born at Windsor lose all: 200
Which is so plain that Exeter doth wish
His days may finish ere that hapless time.   *Exit.*

[Scene 2. *France. Before Rouen.*]

*Enter [La] Pucelle disguised, with four Soldiers
with sacks upon their backs.*

Pucelle. These are the city gates, the gates of Rouen,
   Through which our policy° must make a breach.
   Take heed, be wary how you place your words;
   Talk like the vulgar° sort of market men°
   That come to gather money for their corn.°   5
   If we have entrance, as I hope we shall,
   And that we find the slothful watch but weak,
   I'll by a sign give notice to our friends
   That Charles the Dolphin may encounter° them.

Soldier. Our sacks shall be a mean° to sack the city,   10
   And we be lords and rulers over Rouen;
   Therefore we'll knock.   *Knock.*

Watchman. [*Within*] *Qui est là?*°

Pucelle. Paysans là, pauvres gens de France:°
   Poor market folks that come to sell their corn.   15

Watchman. Enter, go in, the market bell is rung.

Pucelle. Now, Rouen, I'll shake thy bulwarks to the
   ground.   *Exeunt.*

198 **sucking** nursing   3.2.2 **policy** stratagem   4 **vulgar** common
4 **market men** people going to market 5 **corn** grain 9 **encounter**
assail 10 **mean** means 13 **Qui est là** who is there? 14 **Paysans**
. . . **France** peasants here, poor folk of France

Enter Charles [the Dauphin], Bastard, Alençon,
[Reignier, and forces].

Dauphin. Saint Denis bless this happy stratagem,
    And once again we'll sleep secure in Rouen!

20 *Bastard.* Here entered Pucelle and her practisants.°
    Now she is there, how will she specify:
    Here is the best and safest passage in?

Reignier. By thrusting out a torch from yonder tower,
    Which, once discerned, shows that her meaning is:
25 No way to° that, for weakness, which she entered.

Enter [La] Pucelle on the top, thrusting out a
torch burning.

Pucelle. Behold, this is the happy wedding torch
    That joineth Rouen unto her countrymen,
    But burning fatal to the Talbonites!°   [*Exit.*]

Bastard. See, noble Charles, the beacon of our friend,
30 The burning torch, in yonder turret stands.

Dauphin. Now shine it° like a comet of revenge,
    A prophet to the fall of all our foes!

Reignier. Defer° no time, delays have dangerous
    ends;
    Enter and cry, "The Dolphin!" presently,
35 And then do execution on the watch.

                                    Alarum. [*Exeunt.*]

An alarum. Talbot in an excursion.°

Talbot. France, thou shalt rue this treason with thy
    tears,
    If Talbot but survive thy treachery.
    Pucelle, that witch, that damnèd sorceress,
    Hath wrought this hellish mischief unawares,
40 That hardly we escaped the pride° of France.

                                            Exit.

20 **practisants** companions in the stratagem   25 **to** comparable to
28 **Talbonites** followers of Talbot   31 **shine it** may it shine   33
Defer waste   35s.d. **excursion** sortie   40 **pride** finest warriors

An alarum: excursions. Bedford, brought in sick in
a chair. Enter Talbot and Burgundy without: within
[La] Pucelle, Charles [the Dauphin], Bastard,
[Alençon,] and Reignier on the walls.

Pucelle. Good morrow, gallants!° Want ye corn for
    bread?
  I think the Duke of Burgundy will fast
  Before he'll buy again at such a rate.
  'Twas full of darnel;° do you like the taste?

Burgundy. Scoff on, vile fiend and shameless
    courtesan!°   45
  I trust ere long to choke thee with thine own
  And make thee curse the harvest of that corn.

Dauphin. Your grace may starve perhaps before that
    time.

Bedford. O, let no words, but deeds, revenge this
    treason!

Pucelle. What will you do, good gray-beard? Break
    a lance,   50
  And run a-tilt° at death within a chair?

Talbot. Foul fiend of France, and hag of all despite,°
  Encompassed° with thy lustful paramours!°
  Becomes it thee to taunt his valiant age
  And twit° with cowardice a man half dead?   55
  Damsel,° I'll have a bout with you again,
  Or else let Talbot perish with this shame.

Pucelle. Are ye so hot,° sir? Yet, Pucelle, hold thy
    peace;
  If Talbot do but thunder, rain will follow.

    [The English] whisper together in council.

  God speed the parliament! who shall be the
    Speaker?°   60

41 **gallants** gentlemen 44 **darnel** weeds 45 **courtesan** prostitute
50–51 **Break . . . a-tilt** joust, combat 52 **of all despite** full of malice 53 **Encompassed** surrounded 53 **paramours** lovers 55 **twit**
chide 56 **Damsel** girl 58 **hot** angry 60 **Speaker** presiding officer

Talbot. Dare ye come forth and meet us in the field?

Pucelle. Belike° your lordship takes us then for fools,
　　To try if that our own be ours or no.

Talbot. I speak not to that railing Hecate,°
65　　But unto thee, Alençon, and the rest.
　　Will ye, like soldiers, come and fight it out?

Alençon. Signior,° no.

Talbot. Signior, hang! base muleters° of France!
　　Like peasant foot-boys° do they keep the walls
70　　And dare not take up arms like gentlemen.

Pucelle. Away, captains! let's get us from the walls;
　　For Talbot means no goodness by his looks.
　　Good-bye, my lord! we came but to tell you
　　That we are here.　　　　　*Exeunt from the walls.*

75 *Talbot.* And there will we be too, ere it be long,
　　Or else reproach be Talbot's greatest fame.
　　Vow, Burgundy, by honor of thy house,
　　Pricked on° by public wrongs sustained in France,
　　Either to get the town again or die.
80　　And I, as sure as English Henry lives
　　And as his father here was conqueror,
　　As sure as in this late-betrayèd town
　　Great Cordelion's° heart was burièd,
　　So sure I swear to get° the town or die.

85 *Burgundy.* My vows are equal partners with thy vows.

Talbot. But, ere we go, regard° this dying prince,
　　The valiant Duke of Bedford. Come, my lord,
　　We will bestow you in some better place,
　　Fitter for sickness and for crazy° age.

90 *Bedford.* Lord Talbot, do not so dishonor me;
　　Here will I sit before the walls of Rouen

---

62 **Belike** perhaps　64 **railing Hecate** abusive witch (after Hecate,
goddess of sorcery)　67 **Signior** sir　68 **muleters** mule-drivers
69 **foot-boys** boy-servants　78 **Pricked on** provoked　83 **Cordelion's** King Richard the Lion-Hearted's　84 **get** retake　86 **regard**
behold　89 **crazy** infirm, decrepit

And will be partner of your weal or woe.°

Burgundy. Courageous Bedford, let us now persuade
　you.

Bedford. Not to be gone from hence, for once I read
　That stout Pendragon° in his litter° sick　　　　　　*95*
　Came to the field and vanquishèd his foes.
　Methinks I should revive the soldiers' hearts,
　Because I ever found them as myself.

Talbot. Undaunted spirit in a dying breast!
　Then be it so: heavens keep old Bedford safe!　　　*100*
　And now no more ado, brave Burgundy,
　But gather we our forces out of hand
　And set upon our boasting enemy.

　　　[Exeunt all but Bedford and his Attendants.]

　　*An alarum: excursions.° Enter Sir John Falstaff
　　　　　　and a Captain.*

Captain. Whither away, Sir John Falstaff, in such
　haste?

Falstaff. Whither away? To save myself by flight;　　*105*
　We are like to have the overthrow° again.

Captain. What! Will you fly, and leave Lord Talbot?

Falstaff.　　　　　　　　　　　　　　　　Ay,
　All the Talbots in the world, to save my life.

　　　　　　　　　　　　　　　　　　　Exit.

Captain. Cowardly knight, ill fortune follow thee!

　　　　　　　　　　　　　　　　　　　Exit.

　　*Retreat. Excursions. [La] Pucelle, Alençon, and
　　　　Charles [the Dauphin enter and] fly.*

Bedford. Now, quiet soul, depart when heaven please,　　*110*

---

92 **weal or woe** good or bad fortune　95 **Pendragon** Uther Pendragon, father of King Arthur　95 **litter** stretcher-bed　103s.d. **excursions** entries and exits of skirmishing troops　106 **have the overthrow** be defeated

For I have seen our enemies' overthrow.
What is the trust or strength of foolish man?
They that of late were daring with their scoffs
Are glad and fain° by flight to save themselves.

Bedford dies and is carried in by two in his chair.

An alarum. Enter Talbot, Burgundy, and the rest
[of their men].

115 *Talbot.* Lost, and recovered in a day again!
This is a double honor, Burgundy;
Yet heavens have glory for this victory!

Burgundy. Warlike and martial Talbot, Burgundy
Enshrines thee in his heart and there erects
120 Thy noble deeds as valor's monuments.

Talbot. Thanks, gentle duke. But where is Pucelle
now?
I think her old familiar° is asleep.
Now where's the Bastard's braves,° and Charles
his gleeks?°
What, all amort?° Rouen hangs her head for grief
125 That such a valiant company are fled.
Now will we take some order° in the town,
Placing therein some expert° officers,
And then depart to Paris to the king,
For there young Henry with his nobles lie.°

130 *Burgundy.* What wills Lord Talbot pleaseth Burgundy.

Talbot. But yet, before we go, let's not forget
The noble Duke of Bedford, late deceased,
But see his exequies° fulfilled in Rouen.
A braver soldier never couchèd° lance,
135 A gentler° heart did never sway° in court.
But kings and mightiest potentates must die,
For that's the end of human misery.   *Exeunt.*

114 **fain** eager   122 **familiar** servant demon   123 **braves** boasts
123 **gleeks** jests, scoffs   124 **amort** dejected   126 **take some order**
restore order   127 **expert** experienced   129 **lie** reside   133 **exe-**
quies funeral ceremonies   134 **couchèd** leveled for the assault   135
gentler nobler   135 **sway** prevail

Scene 3. [*The plains near Rouen.*]

Enter Charles [the Dauphin], Bastard, Alençon, [La]
Pucelle, [and forces].

Pucelle. Dismay not, princes, at this accident,
  Nor grieve that Rouen is so recoverèd.
  Care is no cure, but rather corrosive,°
  For things that are not to be remedied.
  Let frantic° Talbot triumph for a while   5
  And like a peacock sweep along his tail;
  We'll pull° his plumes and take away his train,°
  If Dolphin and the rest will be but ruled.°

Dauphin. We have been guided by thee hitherto
  And of thy cunning had no diffidence;°   10
  One sudden foil° shall never breed distrust.

Bastard. Search out thy wit° for secret policies,
  And we will make thee famous through the world.

Alençon. We'll set thy statue in some holy place,
  And have thee reverenced like a blessèd saint.   15
  Employ thee° then, sweet virgin, for our good.

Pucelle. Then thus it must be; this doth Joan devise:°
  By fair persuasions mixed with sugared° words
  We will entice the Duke of Burgundy
  To leave the Talbot and to follow us.   20

Dauphin. Ay, marry, sweeting,° if we could do that,
  France were no place for Henry's warriors,

3.3.3 **corrosive** a caustic drug   5 **frantic** raging   7 **pull** pluck
7 **train** (1) followers (2) equipment for battle   8 **ruled** guided (by
Joan)   10 **diffidence** lack of confidence   11 **foil** defeat   12 **Search
out thy wit** examine your mind   16 **Employ thee** apply your efforts   17 **devise** determine   18 **sugared** sweet-sounding   21 **sweeting** sweetheart

Nor should that nation boast it so with° us,
But be extirpèd° from our provinces.

Alençon. Forever should they be expulsed° from
25   France
And not have title of° an earldom here.

Pucelle. Your honors shall perceive how I will work
To bring this matter to the wishèd end.

                    Drum sounds afar off.

Hark! by the sound of drum you may perceive
30   Their powers are marching unto Paris-ward.°

                Here sound an English march.

There goes the Talbot, with his colors spread,°
And all the troops of English after him.

French march. [*Enter the Duke of Burgundy and
                    forces.*]

Now in the rearward comes the duke and his;
Fortune in favor° makes him lag behind.
35   Summon a parley; we will talk with him.

                    Trumpets sound a parley.

Dauphin. A parley with the Duke of Burgundy!

Burgundy. Who craves a parley with the Burgundy?

Pucelle. The princely Charles of France, thy
      countryman.

Burgundy. What say'st thou, Charles? For I am
      marching hence.

Dauphin. Speak, Pucelle, and enchant him with thy
40   words.

Pucelle. Brave Burgundy, undoubted hope of France!
      Stay, let thy humble handmaid speak to thee.

Burgundy. Speak on, but be not over-tedious.

23 **boast it so with** lord it over   24 **extirpèd** rooted out   25 **expulsed**
driven out   26 **title of** claim to   30 **unto Paris-ward** toward Paris
31 **colors spread** banners unfurled   34 **in favor** to our advantage

Pucelle. Look on thy country, look on fertile France,
 And see the cities and the towns defaced   45
 By wasting ruin of the cruel foe,
 As looks the mother on her lowly babe
 When death doth close his tender-dying° eyes.
 See, see the pining° malady of France;
 Behold the wounds, the most unnatural wounds, 50
 Which thou thyself hast given her woeful breast.
 O, turn thy edgèd° sword another way;
 Strike those that hurt, and hurt not those that help.
 One drop of blood drawn from thy country's bosom
 Should grieve thee more than streams of foreign
  gore.   55
 Return thee therefore with a flood of tears,
 And wash away thy country's stainèd° spots.

Burgundy. Either she hath bewitched me with her
 words,
 Or nature makes me suddenly relent.

Pucelle. Besides, all French and France exclaims on°
 thee,   60
 Doubting thy birth and lawful progeny.°
 Who join'st thou with, but with a lordly° nation
 That will not trust thee but for profit's sake?
 When Talbot hath set footing° once in France
 And fashioned thee° that instrument of ill, 65
 Who then but English Henry will be lord,
 And thou be thrust out like a fugitive?
 Call we to mind, and mark but this for proof:
 Was not the Duke of Orleans thy foe?
 And was he not in England prisoner? 70
 But when they heard he was thine enemy,
 They set him free without his ransom paid,
 In spite of Burgundy and all his friends.
 See then, thou fight'st against thy countrymen

---

48 **tender-dying** prematurely dying 49 **pining** consuming 52
edgèd sharp 57 **stainèd** disgraceful 60 **exclaims on** cries out
against 61 **lawful progeny** legitimate parentage 62 **lordly** imperious, disdainful 64 **set footing** entered 65 **fashioned thee** made
you into

75   And join'st with them will be thy slaughter-men.°
        Come, come, return; return, thou wandering lord;
        Charles and the rest will take thee in their arms.

Burgundy. I am vanquishèd; these haughty° words of
        hers
        Have battered me like roaring cannon-shot,
80   And made me almost yield upon my knees.
        Forgive me, country, and sweet countrymen,
        And, lords, accept this hearty kind° embrace.
        My forces and my power of men° are yours.
        So farewell, Talbot; I'll no longer trust thee.

Pucelle. [*Aside*] Done like a Frenchman: turn and
85   turn again!°

Dauphin. Welcome, brave duke! thy friendship makes
        us fresh.°

Bastard. And doth beget new courage in our breasts.

Alençon. Pucelle hath bravely played her part in this,
        And doth deserve a coronet° of gold.

Dauphin. Now let us on, my lords, and join our
90   powers,
        And seek how we may prejudice° the foe.   *Exeunt.*

75 **slaughter-men** executioners 78 **haughty** loftily brave 82 **kind**
(1) friendly (2) of a kinsman 83 **my power of men** (1) my full com-
plement of troops (?) (2) command over my troops 85 **turn and
turn again** change sides frequently 86 **makes us fresh** renews our
spirits 89 **coronet** a small crown worn on state occasions by members of the nobility 91 **prejudice** damage

Scene 4. [*Paris. The Palace.*]

Enter the King, Gloucester, Winchester, York, Suf-
folk, Somerset, Warwick, Exeter, [Vernon, Basset,
and others]. To them, with his Soldiers, Talbot.

Talbot. My gracious prince, and honorable peers,
 Hearing of your arrival in this realm,
 I have awhile given truce unto my wars
 To do my duty to my sovereign.
 In sign whereof, this arm, that hath reclaimed°   5
 To your obedience fifty fortresses,
 Twelve cities, and seven wallèd towns of strength,
 Beside five hundred prisoners of esteem,°
 Lets fall his sword before your highness' feet,
 And with submissive loyalty of heart   10
 Ascribes the glory of his conquest got
 First to my God and next unto your grace.

King. Is this the Lord Talbot, uncle Gloucester,
 That hath so long been resident in France?

Gloucester. Yes, if it please your majesty, my liege.°   15

King. Welcome, brave captain and victorious lord!
 When I was young (as yet I am not old)
 I do remember° how my father said
 A stouter champion never handled sword.
 Long since we were resolvèd of your truth,°   20
 Your faithful service, and your toil in war;
 Yet never have you tasted our reward
 Or been reguerdoned° with so much as thanks,

3.4.5 **reclaimed** subdued   8 **esteem** good reputation in battle and
high birth (thus likely to command a profitable ransom)   15 **liege**
sovereign lord   18 **remember** (but Henry VI was only nine months
old when his father died)   20 **resolvèd of your truth** convinced of
your loyalty   23 **reguerdoned** repaid

Because till now we never saw your face.
25   Therefore, stand up, and for these good deserts
We here create you Earl of Shrewsbury,
And in our coronation take your place.

Sennet. Flourish. Exeunt. Manet° Vernon and Basset.

Vernon. Now, sir, to you, that were so hot° at sea,
Disgracing of° these colors that I wear
30   In honor of my noble Lord of York—
Dar'st   thou   maintain   the   former   words   thou
spak'st?

Basset. Yes, sir, as well as you dare patronage°
The envious barking of your saucy tongue
Against my lord the Duke of Somerset.

35   *Vernon.* Sirrah, thy lord I honor as he is.

Basset. Why, what is he? As good a man as York.

Vernon. Hark ye, not so: in witness,° take ye that.

Strikes him.

Basset. Villain, thou knowest the law of arms is such
That whoso draws a sword,° 'tis present° death,
40   Or else this blow should broach° thy dearest blood.
But I'll unto his majesty and crave°
I may have liberty to venge° this wrong.
When thou shalt see I'll meet thee to thy cost.

Vernon. Well, miscreant,° I'll be there as soon as
you,
45   And, after, meet you sooner than you would.

Exeunt.

27s.d. **Manet** remains (the Latin singular with a plural subject is
common in Elizabethan stage directions)   28 **hot** passionate   29
Disgracing of disparaging   32 **patronage** (1) maintain (2) defend
37 **in witness** as proof   39 **draws a sword** i.e., in a royal residence
39 **present** immediate   40 **broach** draw as with a tap   41 **crave**
beg   42 **venge** avenge   44 **miscreant** coward

ACT 4

Scene 1. [*Paris. A hall of state.*]

Enter King, Gloucester, Winchester, York, Suffolk, Somerset, Warwick, Talbot, Exeter, Governor [of Paris and others].

Gloucester. Lord bishop, set the crown upon his head.

Winchester. God save King Henry, of that name the sixth!

Gloucester. Now, governor of Paris, take your oath,
That you elect no other king but him;
Esteem none friends but such as are his friends,   5
And none your foes but such as shall pretend°
Malicious practices° against his state:
This shall ye do, so help you righteous God!

Enter Falstaff.

Falstaff. My gracious sovereign, as I rode from Calais
To haste unto your coronation,   10
A letter was delivered to my hands,
Writ to your grace from th' Duke of Burgundy.

4.1.6 **pretend** purpose 7 **practices** stratagems

Talbot. Shame to the Duke of Burgundy and thee!
 I vowed, base knight, when I did meet thee next,
15 To tear the garter° from thy craven's° leg,

      [Plucking it off.]

 Which I have done, because unworthily
 Thou wast installèd in that high degree.°
 Pardon me, princely Henry, and the rest:
 This dastard, at the battle of Poictiers,°
20 When but in all I was six thousand strong
 And that the French were almost ten to one,
 Before we met or that a stroke was given,
 Like to a trusty squire° did run away.
 In which assault we lost twelve hundred men;
25 Myself and divers gentlemen beside
 Were there surprised and taken prisoners.
 Then judge, great lords, if I have done amiss,
 Or whether that such cowards ought to wear
 This ornament of knighthood, yea or no.

30 *Gloucester.* To say the truth, this fact° was infamous
 And ill beseeming any common man,
 Much more a knight, a captain, and a leader.

Talbot. When first this order was ordained, my lords,
 Knights of the Garter were of noble birth,
35 Valiant and virtuous, full of haughty° courage,
 Such as were grown to credit° by the wars;
 Not fearing death, nor shrinking for distress,°
 But always resolute in most extremes.°
 He then that is not furnished in this sort°
40 Doth but usurp the sacred name of knight,
 Profaning this most honorable order,
 And should (if I were worthy to be judge)

---

15 **garter** badge of the Order of the Garter, England's highest degree of knighthood 15 **craven's** coward's 17 **degree** dignity 19
Poictiers i.e., Patay (1429) 23 **trusty squire** (used contemptuously:
a person of inferior character) 30 **fact** deed 35 **haughty** high
36 **credit** honorable reputation 37 **distress** adversity 38 **in most
extremes** in the most difficult situations 39 **furnished in this sort**
possessed of such qualities

Be quite degraded, like a hedge-born swain°
That doth presume to boast of gentle blood.

King. Stain to thy countrymen, thou hear'st
    thy doom!°   45
Be packing,° therefore, thou that wast a knight:
Henceforth we banish thee on pain of death.

[*Exit Falstaff.*]

And now, Lord Protector, view the letter
Sent from our uncle Duke of Burgundy.

Gloucester. What means his grace, that he hath
    changed his style?°   50
No more but plain and bluntly, "To the king!"
Hath he forgot he is his sovereign?
Or doth this churlish superscription
Pretend° some alteration in good will?
What's here? "I have, upon especial cause,   55
Moved with compassion of my country's wrack,°
Together with the pitiful complaints
Of such as your oppression feeds upon,
Forsaken your pernicious faction
And joined with Charles, the rightful King of
    France."   60
O monstrous treachery! can this be so,
That in alliance, amity, and oaths,
There should be found such false dissembling
    guile?

King. What! doth my uncle Burgundy revolt?

Gloucester. He doth, my lord, and is become your foe.   65

King. Is that the worst this letter doth contain?

Gloucester. It is the worst, and all, my lord, he writes.

King. Why, then, Lord Talbot there shall talk with
    him

---

43 **hedge-born swain** low peasant 45 **doom** judgment, condemnation 46 **Be packing** begone 50 **style** form of address 54 **Pretend** signify 56 **wrack** misfortune

And give him chastisement for this abuse.
70   How say you, my lord; are you not content?

Talbot. Content, my liege? Yes, but that I am prevented,°
I should have begged I might have been employed.

King. Then gather strength, and march unto him
straight;
Let him perceive how ill we brook° his treason
75   And what offense it is to flout his friends.

Talbot. I go, my lord, in heart desiring still
You may behold confusion of your foes.   [*Exit.*]

Enter Vernon and Basset.

Vernon. Grant me the combat,° gracious sovereign.

Basset. And me, my lord, grant me the combat too.

80   *York.* This is my servant; hear him, noble prince.

Somerset. And this is mine; sweet Henry, favor him.

King. Be patient, lords, and give them leave to
speak.
Say, gentlemen, what makes you thus exclaim,
And wherefore crave you combat? Or with whom?

Vernon. With him, my lord, for he hath done me
85   wrong.

Basset. And I with him, for he hath done me wrong.

King. What is that wrong whereof you both complain?
First let me know, and then I'll answer you.

Basset. Crossing the sea from England into France,
90   This fellow here, with envious carping° tongue,
Upbraided° me about the rose I wear,
Saying, the sanguine° color of the leaves

_____

71 **prevented** anticipated 74 **brook** bear with 78 **combat** trial by
arms 90 **carping** fault-finding 91 **Upbraided** reproached 92
sanguine bloodred

Did represent my master's blushing cheeks,
When stubbornly he did repugn° the truth
About a certain question in the law	95
Argued betwixt the Duke of York and him;
With other vile and ignominious terms;
In confutation of which rude reproach
And in defense of my lord's worthiness,
I crave the benefit of law of arms.°	100

Vernon. And that is my petition, noble lord:
For though he seem with forgèd quaint conceit°
To set a gloss upon° his bold intent,
Yet know, my lord, I was provoked by him,
And he first took exceptions at° this badge,	105
Pronouncing that the paleness of this flower
Bewrayed° the faintness of my master's heart.

York. Will not this malice, Somerset, be left?

Somerset. Your private grudge, my Lord of York, will
out,
Though ne'er so cunningly you smother it.	110

King. Good Lord, what madness rules in brain-
sick men,
When for so slight and frivolous a cause
Such factious emulations° shall arise!
Good cousins both, of York and Somerset,
Quiet yourselves, I pray, and be at peace.	115

York. Let this dissension first be tried by fight,
And then your highness shall command a peace.

Somerset. The quarrel toucheth° none but us alone;
Betwixt ourselves let us decide it then.

York. There is my pledge;° accept it, Somerset.	120

Vernon. Nay, let it rest where it began at first.

94 **repugn** resist 100 **benefit . . . arms** privilege of trial by combat
102 **forgèd quaint conceit** crafty manner of expression 103 **set a
gloss upon** veil in specious language 105 **took exceptions at** disap-
proved of 107 **Bewrayed** revealed 113 **emulations** contentions
118 **toucheth** concerns 120 **pledge** challenge (made by casting
down one's glove)

Basset. Confirm it so, mine honorable lord.

Gloucester. Confirm it so? Confounded be your strife!
  And perish ye with your audacious prate!°
125 Presumptuous vassals, are you not ashamed
  With this immodest° clamorous outrage
  To trouble and disturb the king and us?
  And you, my lords, methinks you do not well
  To bear with their perverse objections,
130 Much less to take occasion from their mouths
  To raise a mutiny betwixt yourselves.
  Let me persuade you take a better course.

Exeter. It grieves his highness. Good my lords, be
  friends.

King. Come hither, you that would be com-
  batants:
135 Henceforth I charge you, as you love our favor,
  Quite to forget this quarrel and the cause.
  And you, my lords, remember where we are:
  In France, amongst a fickle wavering nation;
  If they perceive dissension in our looks
140 And that within ourselves we disagree,
  How will their grudging stomachs° be provoked
  To wilful disobedience, and rebel!
  Beside, what infamy will there arise,
  When foreign princes shall be certified°
145 That for a toy,° a thing of no regard,
  King Henry's peers and chief nobility
  Destroyed themselves and lost the realm of France!
  O, think upon the conquest of my father,
  My tender years, and let us not forgo
150 That for a trifle that was bought with blood!
  Let me be umpire in this doubtful strife.
  I see no reason, if I wear this rose,

  [*Putting on a red rose.*]

That anyone should therefore be suspicious

---

124 **prate** chatter 126 **immodest** arrogant 141 **grudging stomachs**
resentful dispositions 144 **certified** informed 145 **toy** trifle

I more incline to Somerset than York;
Both are my kinsmen, and I love them both.   155
As well they may upbraid me with my crown
Because, forsooth,° the King of Scots is crowned.
But your discretions° better can persuade
Than I am able to instruct or teach,
And therefore, as we hither came in peace,   160
So let us still continue peace and love.
Cousin of York, we institute your grace
To be our Regent in these parts of France;
And, good my Lord of Somerset, unite
Your troops of horsemen with his bands of foot,   165
And, like true subjects, sons of your progenitors,
Go cheerfully together and digest
Your angry choler° on your enemies.
Ourself, my Lord Protector, and the rest
After some respite will return to Calais;   170
From thence to England, where I hope ere long
To be presented, by your victories,
With Charles, Alençon, and that traitorous rout.°

> *Flourish. Exeunt. Manet York, Warwick,*
> *Exeter, Vernon.*

Warwick. My Lord of York, I promise you, the king
Prettily, methought, did play the orator.   175

York. And so he did, but yet I like it not,
In that he wears the badge of Somerset.

Warwick. Tush, that was but his fancy, blame him
not;
I dare presume, sweet prince, he thought no harm.

York. And if—I wish—he did. But let it rest;   180
Other affairs must now be managèd.

> *Exeunt. Manet Exeter.*

---

157 **forsooth** in truth (used derisively) 158 **discretions** lordships,
judgments 168 **choler** bile (according to earlier physiology, the
cause of anger or hot temper) 173 **rout** crowd

Exeter. Well didst thou, Richard, to suppress thy
          voice;
     For, had the passions of thy heart burst out,
     I fear we should have seen deciphered° there
185 More rancorous spite, more furious raging broils,
     Than yet can be imagined or supposed.
     But howsoe'er, no simple man that sees
     This jarring discord of nobility,
     This shouldering° of each other in the court,
190 This factious bandying° of their favorites,
     But that it doth presage some ill event.°
     'Tis much° when scepters are in children's hands,
     But more when envy breeds unkind division;°
     There comes the ruin, there begins confusion.   *Exit.*

[Scene 2.] *Before Bordeaux.*

Enter Talbot, with trump and drum.

Talbot. Go to the gates of Bordeaux, trumpeter;
     Summon their general unto the wall.

                         [*Trumpet*] *sounds.*

Enter General aloft [with others].

     English John Talbot, captains, calls you forth,
     Servant in arms to Harry King of England,
5   And thus he would: open your city gates,
     Be humble to us, call my sovereign yours
     And do him homage as obedient subjects,
     And I'll withdraw me and my bloody power.
     But, if you frown upon this proffered peace,
10   You tempt the fury of my three attendants,

184 **deciphered** revealed   189 **shouldering** jostling   190 **bandying**
contention   191 **presage some ill event** predict some evil outcome
192 **much** difficult   193 **unkind division** unnatural disunion

Lean Famine, quartering° Steel, and climbing Fire,
Who in a moment even° with the earth
Shall lay your stately and air-braving° towers,
If you forsake the offer of their love.

General. Thou ominous and fearful owl of death,°   15
Our nation's terror and their bloody scourge!
The period° of thy tyranny approacheth.
On us thou canst not enter but by death,
For, I protest, we are well fortified
And strong enough to issue out and fight.   20
If thou retire, the Dolphin, well appointed,°
Stands with the snares of war to tangle thee.
On either hand° thee there are squadrons pitched
To wall thee from the liberty of flight,
And no way canst thou turn thee for redress,°   25
But death doth front° thee with apparent spoil,°
And pale destruction meets thee in the face.
Ten thousand French have ta'en the sacrament°
To rive° their dangerous artillery
Upon no Christian soul but English Talbot.   30
Lo, there thou stand'st, a breathing valiant man,
Of an invincible unconquered spirit!
This is the latest° glory of thy praise
That I, thy enemy, due° thee withal,
For ere the glass that now begins to run   35
Finish the process of his sandy hour,
These eyes, that see thee now well colorèd,°
Shall see thee withered, bloody, pale, and dead.

                              Drum afar off.

Hark! hark! The Dolphin's drum, a warning bell,
Sings heavy° music to thy timorous soul,   40

4.2.11 **quartering** that cuts men into quarters 12 **even** level 13
air-braving skyscraping 15 **owl of death** (alluding to the owl as a
supposed harbinger of death or misfortune) 17 **period** end 21
appointed equipped 23 **hand** side of 25 **redress** relief 26 **front**
confront 26 **apparent spoil** obvious destruction 28 **ta'en the
sacrament** confirmed their oaths by receiving holy communion
29 **rive** burst 33 **latest** final 34 **due** endue 37 **well colorèd** of
healthy complexion 40 **heavy** doleful

And mine shall ring thy dire departure out.

Exit [with his followers].

Talbot. He fables not,° I hear the enemy;
    Out, some light° horsemen, and peruse their wings.°
    O, negligent and heedless discipline!
45   How are we parked and bounded in a pale,°
    A little herd of England's timorous deer,
    Mazed with° a yelping kennel of French curs!
    If we be English deer, be then in blood,°
    Not rascal-like° to fall down with a pinch,°
50   But rather moody-mad;° and, desperate stags,
    Turn on the bloody° hounds with heads of steel
    And make the cowards stand aloof at bay.
    Sell every man his life as dear as mine,
    And they shall find dear° deer of us, my friends.
55   God and Saint George, Talbot and England's right,
    Prosper our colors in this dangerous fight!   *[Exeunt.]*

[Scene 3. *Plains in Gascony*.]

*Enter a Messenger that meets York. Enter York with
trumpet and many Soldiers.*

York. Are not the speedy scouts returned again
    That dogged° the mighty army of the Dolphin?

Messenger. They are returned, my lord, and give it
    out°
    That he is marched to Bordeaux with his power
5   To fight with Talbot. As he marched along,
    By your espials° were discoverèd

---

42 **fables not** does not speak falsely   43 **light** lightly armed   43
peruse their wings scout their flanks   45 **parked . . . pale** surrounded and hemmed in by a fence   47 **Mazed with** terrified by
48 **in blood** (1) in full vigor (2) in temper   49 **rascal-like** like inferior deer   49 **pinch** nip   50 **moody-mad** furious in mood   51
bloody bloodthirsty   54 **dear** costly   4.3.2 **dogged** tracked, closely
pursued   3 **give it out** report   6 **espials** spies

Two mightier troops than that the Dolphin led,
Which joined with him and made their march for
   Bordeaux.

York. A plague upon that villain Somerset,
That thus delays my promisèd supply   *10*
Of horsemen that were levied for this siege!
Renownèd Talbot doth expect° my aid,
And I am louted° by a traitor villain
And cannot help the noble chevalier.°
God comfort him in this necessity!   *15*
If he miscarry,° farewell wars in France.

   Enter another Messenger: [Sir William Lucy.]

Lucy. Thou princely leader of our English strength,
Never so needful on the earth of France,
Spur to the rescue of the noble Talbot,
Who now is girdled with a waist of iron   *20*
And hemmed about with grim destruction.
To Bordeaux, warlike duke! to Bordeaux, York!
Else, farewell Talbot, France, and England's honor.

York. O God, that Somerset, who in proud heart
Doth stop my cornets,° were in Talbot's place!   *25*
So should we save a valiant gentleman
By forfeiting a traitor and a coward.
Mad ire and wrathful fury make me weep,
That thus we die, while remiss traitors sleep.

Lucy. O, send some succor to the distressed lord!   *30*

York. He dies, we lose; I break my warlike word;
We mourn, France smiles; we lose, they daily get;
All long° of this vile traitor Somerset.

Lucy. Then God take mercy on brave Talbot's soul,
And on his son young John, who two hours since   *35*
I met in travel toward his warlike father!
This seven years did not Talbot see his son,
And now they meet where both their lives are done.

12 **expect** await 13 **louted** mocked 14 **chevalier** knight 16 **miscarry** be destroyed 25 **stop my cornets** withhold my squadrons of cavalry 33 **long** on account

York. Alas, what joy shall noble Talbot have
40   To bid his young son welcome to his grave?
       Away! vexation almost stops my breath,
       That sundered° friends greet in the hour of death.
       Lucy, farewell, no more my fortune can°
       But curse the cause° I cannot aid the man.
45   Maine, Blois, Poictiers, and Tours are won away,
       Long all of Somerset and his delay.

                          Exit [with his Soldiers].

Lucy. Thus, while the vulture of sedition
       Feeds in the bosom of such great commanders,
       Sleeping neglection° doth betray to loss
50   The conquest of our scarce-cold° conqueror,
       That ever living man of memory,
       Henry the Fifth. Whiles they each other cross,
       Lives, honors, lands, and all hurry to loss.

          [Scene 4. *Other plains in Gascony.*]

       *Enter Somerset with his army, [a Captain of Talbot's
                          with him].*

Somerset. It is too late, I cannot send them now;
       This expedition was by York and Talbot
       Too rashly plotted. All our general° force
       Might with a sally° of the very° town
5   Be buckled with. The over-daring Talbot
       Hath sullied all his gloss° of former honor
       By this unheedful, desperate, wild adventure;
       York set him on to fight and die in shame,
       That, Talbot dead, great York might bear the name.

42 **sundered** separated   43 **fortune can** circumstances enable me to
do   44 **cause** reason why   49 **neglection** negligence   50 **scarce-cold**
barely dead   4.4.3 **general** whole   4 **sally** sudden outrush   4 **very**
itself   6 **gloss** luster

Captain. Here is Sir William Lucy, who with me   10
    Set from our o'er-matched° forces forth for aid.

Somerset. How now, Sir William! whither were you
    sent?

Lucy. Whither, my lord? from bought and sold Lord
    Talbot;
    Who, ringed about with bold adversity,°
    Cries out for noble York and Somerset   15
    To beat assailing death from his weak regions;°
    And whiles the honorable captain there
    Drops bloody sweat from his war-wearied limbs,
    And in advantage ling'ring° looks for rescue,
    You, his false hopes, the trust of England's honor,   20
    Keep off aloof with worthless emulation.°
    Let not your private discord keep away
    The levied succors° that should lend him aid
    While he, renownèd noble gentleman,
    Yield up his life unto a world of odds: 25
    Orleans the Bastard, Charles, Burgundy,
    Alençon, Reignier compass him about,
    And Talbot perisheth by your default.

Somerset. York set him on, York should have sent
    him aid.

Lucy. And York as fast upon your grace exclaims,   30
    Swearing that you withhold his levied host,
    Collected for this expedition.

Somerset. York lies; he might have sent and had the
    horse!
    I owe him little duty, and less love,
    And take° foul scorn to fawn on him by sending.   35

Lucy. The fraud of England, not the force of France,
    Hath now entrapped the noble-minded Talbot;

---

11 **o'er-matched** outnumbered   14 **bold adversity** confident op-
ponents   16 **regions** places   19 **in advantage ling'ring** (1) desper-
ately clinging to every advantage (?) (2) while holding out on
advantageous ground (?)   21 **emulation** rivalry   23 **succors** rein-
forcements   35 **take** submit to

Never to England shall he bear his life,
But dies betrayed to fortune by your strife.

Somerset. Come, go; I will dispatch the horsemen
40   straight;
Within six hours they will be at his aid.

Lucy. Too late comes rescue, he is ta'en or slain,
For fly he could not, if he would have fled,
And fly would Talbot never though he might.

45 *Somerset.* If he be dead, brave Talbot, then adieu!

Lucy. His fame lives in the world, his shame in you.
                              Exeunt.

[Scene 5. *The English camp near Bordeaux.*]

Enter Talbot and his son.

Talbot. O young John Talbot! I did send for thee
To tutor thee in stratagems of war,
That Talbot's name might be in thee revived
When sapless° age and weak unable° limbs
5   Should bring thy father to his drooping chair.°
But, O malignant and ill-boding stars!
Now thou art come unto a feast of death,
A terrible and unavoided° danger:
Therefore, dear boy, mount on my swiftest horse,
10   And I'll direct thee how thou shalt escape
By sudden flight. Come, dally not, be gone.

John. Is my name Talbot? And am I your son?
And shall I fly? O, if you love my mother,
Dishonor not her honorable name,
15   To make a bastard and a slave of me.

4.5.4 **sapless** withered   4 **unable** powerless   5 **drooping chair** decline from vigor   8 **unavoided** unavoidable

The world will say, he is not Talbot's blood,
That basely fled when noble Talbot stood.

Talbot. Fly, to revenge my death, if I be slain.

John. He that flies so will ne'er return again.

Talbot. If we both stay, we both are sure to die.   20

John. Then let me stay, and, father, do you fly:
Your loss is great, so your regard should be;
My worth unknown, no loss is known in me.
Upon my death the French can little boast;   25
In yours they will, in you all hopes are lost.
Flight cannot stain the honor you have won,
But mine it will, that no exploit have done;
You fled for vantage,° everyone will swear,
But, if I bow,° they'll say it was for fear.   30
There is no hope that ever I will stay
If the first hour I shrink and run away.
Here on my knee I beg mortality,°
Rather than life preserved with infamy.

Talbot. Shall all thy mother's hopes lie in one tomb?

John. Ay, rather than I'll shame my mother's womb.   35

Talbot. Upon my blessing, I command thee go.

John. To fight I will, but not to fly the foe.

Talbot. Part of thy father may be saved in thee.

John. No part of him but will be shame in me.

Talbot. Thou never hadst renown, nor canst not lose
it.   40

John. Yes, your renownèd name: shall flight abuse it?

Talbot. Thy father's charge° shall clear thee from that
stain.

John. You cannot witness for me, being slain.
If death be so apparent, then both fly.

28 **for vantage** to gain a tactical advantage 29 **bow** flee 32 **mortality** death 42 **charge** attack

45 *Talbot.* And leave my followers here to fight and die?
        My age was never tainted with such shame.

    John. And shall my youth be guilty of such blame?
        No more can I be severed from your side
        Than can yourself yourself in twain° divide.
50   Stay, go, do what you will, the like do I;
        For live I will not, if my father die.

    Talbot. Then here I take my leave of thee, fair son,
        Born to eclipse° thy life this afternoon.
        Come, side by side together live and die;
55   And soul with soul from France to heaven fly.

                                    Exit [*with Son*].

            [Scene 6. *A field of battle.*]

    *Alarum: excursions, wherein Talbot's Son is hemmed
            about, and Talbot rescues him.*

    Talbot. Saint George and victory! fight, soldiers, fight!
        The Regent hath with Talbot broke his word
        And left us to the rage of France his sword.
        Where is John Talbot? Pause, and take thy breath;
5   I gave thee life and rescued thee from death.

    John. O, twice my father, twice am I thy son!
        The life thou gav'st me first was lost and done,
        Till with thy warlike sword, despite of° fate,
        To my determined° time thou gav'st new date.

    Talbot. When from the Dolphin's crest thy sword
10   struck fire,
        It warmed thy father's heart with proud desire
        Of bold-faced victory. Then leaden° age,
        Quickened° with youthful spleen° and warlike rage,

49 **twain** two   53 **eclipse** end   4.6.8 **despite of** in spite of   9
determined predestined, fated   12 **leaden** spiritless   13 **Quickened**
animated   13 **spleen** high spirits, courage

His over-mounting° spirit and there died,
My Icarus, my blossom, in his pride.

Enter [Soldiers,] with John Talbot, borne.

Servant. O my dear lord, lo, where your son is
borne!

Talbot. Thou antic° death, which laugh'st us here to
scorn,
Anon,° from thy insulting tyranny,
Coupled in bonds of perpetuity,°   20
Two Talbots, wingèd through the lither° sky,
In thy despite shall 'scape mortality.
O thou, whose wounds become hard-favored°
death,
Speak to thy father ere thou yield thy breath!
Brave Death by speaking, whether he will or no;   25
Imagine him a Frenchman and thy foe.
Poor boy! he smiles, methinks, as who should say,
"Had Death been French, then Death had died
today."
Come, come and lay him in his father's arms;
My spirit can no longer bear these harms.   30
Soldiers, adieu! I have what I would have,
Now my old arms are young John Talbot's grave.
                                                Dies.

Enter Charles [the Dauphin], Alençon, Burgundy,
        Bastard, and [La] Pucelle, [with forces].

Dauphin. Had York and Somerset brought rescue in,
We should have found a bloody day of this.

Bastard. How the young whelp of Talbot's, raging
wood,°   35
Did flesh his puny-sword° in Frenchmen's blood!

Pucelle. Once I encountered him, and thus I said:

---

15 **over-mounting** too highly aspiring   18 **antic** (1) grinning (2)
buffoon   19 **Anon** immediately   20 **of perpetuity** eternal   21 **lither**
yielding, pliant   23 **hard-favored** ugly-looking   35 **wood** mad   36
flesh his puny-sword initiate his untried sword in battle

"Thou maiden youth, be vanquished by a maid."
But, with a proud majestical high scorn,
40 He answered thus: "Young Talbot was not born
To be the pillage° of a giglot° wench."
So, rushing in the bowels°of the French,
He left me proudly, as unworthy fight.°

Burgundy. Doubtless he would have made a noble
        knight.
45 See, where he lies inhearsèd° in the arms
Of the most bloody nurser° of his harms!

Bastard. Hew them to pieces, hack their bones
        asunder,
Whose life was England's glory, Gallia's wonder.

Dauphin. O no, forbear! for that which we have fled
50 During the life, let us not wrong it dead.

        Enter Lucy, [attended by a French Herald].

Lucy. Herald, conduct me to the Dolphin's tent,
To know who hath obtained the glory of the day.

Dauphin. On what submissive message art thou sent?

Lucy. Submission, Dolphin! 'Tis a mere French word;
55 We English warriors wot not what it means.
I come to know what prisoners thou hast ta'en
And to survey the bodies of the dead.

Dauphin. For prisoners ask'st thou? Hell our prison
        is.°
But tell me whom thou seek'st.

60 *Lucy.* But where's the great Alcides° of the field,
Valiant Lord Talbot, Earl of Shrewsbury,
Created, for his rare success in arms,
Great Earl of Washford, Waterford, and Valence,
Lord Talbot of Goodrig and Urchinfield,
65 Lord Strange of Blackmere, Lord Verdun of Alton,

41 **pillage** plunder   41 **giglot** wanton   42 **bowels** midst   43 **un-worthy fight** not worthy of fighting with   45 **inhearsèd** enclosed as in a hearse   46 **nurser** fosterer   58 **Hell our prison is** i.e., we kill all our enemies   60 **Alcides** Hercules

Lord Cromwell of Wingfield, Lord Furnival of
　　Sheffield,
The thrice-victorious Lord of Falconbridge,
Knight of the noble order of Saint George,
Worthy Saint Michael, and the Golden Fleece,°
Great Marshal to Henry the Sixth   70
Of all his wars within the realm of France?

Pucelle. Here's a silly stately style° indeed!
The Turk,° that two and fifty kingdoms hath,
Writes not so tedious a style as this.
Him that thou magnifi'st with all these titles   75
Stinking and fly-blown lies here at our feet.

Lucy. Is Tailbot slain, the Frenchmen's only scourge,
Your kingdom's terror and black Nemesis?
O, were mine eyeballs into bullets turned,
That I in rage might shoot them at your faces!   80
O, that I could but call these dead to life,
It were enough to fright the realm of France!
Were but his picture left amongst you here,
It would amaze° the proudest of you all.
Give me their bodies, that I may bear them hence   85
And give them burial as beseems their worth.

Pucelle. I think this upstart is old Talbot's ghost,
He speaks with such a proud commanding spirit.
For God's sake, let him have him; to keep them
　　here,
They would but stink and putrefy the air.   90

Dauphin. Go, take their bodies hence.

Lucy. I'll bear them hence, but from their ashes shall
　　be reared
A phoenix° that shall make all France afeard.°

68–70 **Saint George . . . Saint Michael . . . the Golden Fleece**
chivalric orders of England, France, and the Holy Roman Empire
respectively   72 **stately style** imposing title   73 **The Turk** the Sultan
84 **amaze** stupefy, terrify   93 **phoenix** in mythology, an Arabian
bird that is resurrected from the ashes of its own funeral pyre   93
afeard afraid

   Dauphin. So we be rid of them, do with him what
      thou wilt.
95   And now to Paris, in this conquering vein: °
    All will be ours, now bloody Talbot's slain.

                              Exeunt.

95 **vein** mood

ACT 5

[Scene 1. *London. The palace.*]

Sennet. Enter King, Gloucester, and Exeter.

King. Have you perused the letters from the pope,
   The emperor, and the Earl of Armagnac?

Gloucester. I have, my lord, and their intent is this:
   They humbly sue unto your excellence
   To have a godly peace concluded of   5
   Between the realms of England and of France.

King. How doth your grace affect° their motion?

Gloucester. Well, my good lord, and as the only
   means
   To stop effusion of our Christian blood
   And stablish° quietness on every side.   10

King. Ay, marry, uncle, for I always thought
   It was both impious and unnatural
   That such immanity° and bloody strife
   Should reign among professors of° one faith.

Gloucester. Beside, my lord, the sooner to effect   15
   And surer bind this knot of amity,
   The Earl of Armagnac, near knit° to Charles,
   A man of great authority in France,

5.1.7 **affect** like   10 **stablish** establish   13 **immanity** monstrous
cruelty   14 **professors of** believers in   17 **near knit** closely bound
by blood relationship

           Proffers his only daughter to your grace
20   In marriage, with a large and sumptuous dowry.

King. Marriage, uncle! alas, my years are young,
           And fitter is my study and my books
           Than wanton dalliance with a paramour.°
           Yet call th' ambassadors, and, as you please,
25   So let them have their answers every one:
           I shall be well content with any choice
           Tends to God's glory and my country's weal.

        Enter Winchester [in Cardinal's habit], and three Am-
                bassadors, [one of them a Legate°].

Exeter. What! is my Lord of Winchester installed,
           And called unto a cardinal's degree?
30   Then I perceive that will be verified
           Henry the Fifth did sometime° prophesy:
           "If once he come to be a cardinal,
           He'll make his cap° co-equal with the crown."

King. My lords ambassadors, your several suits°
35   Have been considered and debated on.
           Your purpose is both good and reasonable,
           And therefore are we certainly resolved
           To draw conditions of a friendly peace,
           Which by my Lord of Winchester we mean
40   Shall be transported presently to France.

Gloucester. And for the proffer of my lord your mas-
                ter,°
           I have informed his highness so at large
           As,° liking of the lady's virtuous gifts,
           Her beauty and the value of her dower,°
45   He doth intend she shall be England's queen.

King. In argument and proof of which contract,
           Bear her this jewel, pledge of my affection.

---

23 **wanton . . . paramour** lascivious sport with a mistress 27s.d.
Legate representative of the Pope 31 **sometime** once 33 **cap** red
cardinal's skullcap 34 **several suits** individual requests 41 **master**
i.e., the Count of Armagnac 43 **As** that 44 **dower** marriage set-
tlement

And so, my Lord Protector, see them guarded
And safely brought to Dover, wherein shipped,°
Commit them to the fortune of the sea.　　　　50
　　　　Exeunt [all but Winchester and the Legate].

Winchester. Stay, my Lord Legate; you shall first
　　receive
The sum of money which I promisèd
Should be delivered to his Holiness
For clothing me in these grave ornaments.°

Legate. I will attend upon your lordship's leisure.　　55

Winchester. [*Aside*] Now Winchester will not submit,
　　I trow,
Or be inferior to the proudest peer.
Humphrey of Gloucester, thou shalt well perceive
That, neither in birth or for authority,
The bishop will be overborne by thee.　　　　60
I'll either make thee stoop and bend thy knee,
Or sack this country with a mutiny.°　　　　*Exeunt.*

[Scene 2. *France. Plains in Anjou.*]

*Enter Charles [the Dauphin], Burgundy, Alençon,
Bastard, Reignier, and Joan [la Pucelle, with forces].*

Dauphin. These news, my lords, may cheer our droop-
　　ing spirits:
'Tis said the stout Parisians do revolt
And turn again unto the warlike French.

Alençon. Then march to Paris, royal Charles of
　　France.
And keep not back your powers in dalliance.°　　　　5

Pucelle. Peace be amongst them, if they turn to us;
  Else, ruin combat with their palaces!

Enter Scout.

Scout. Success unto our valiant general,
  And happiness to his accomplices!

Dauphin. What tidings send our scouts? I prithee,
10   speak.

Scout. The English army, that divided was
  Into two parties, is now conjoined° in one,
  And means to give you battle presently.

Dauphin. Somewhat too sudden, sirs, the warning is,
15   But we will presently provide for them.

Burgundy. I trust the ghost of Talbot is not there;
  Now he is gone, my lord, you need not fear.

Pucelle. Of all base passions, fear is most accursed.
  Command the conquest, Charles, it shall be thine;
20   Let Henry fret and all the world repine.°

Dauphin. Then on, my lords, and France be fortunate!
                                        Exeunt.

[Scene 3. *Before Angiers.*]

Alarum. Excursions. Enter Joan la Pucelle.

Pucelle. The Regent° conquers, and the Frenchmen
  fly.
  Now help, ye charming° spells and periapts,°
  And ye choice° spirits that admonish° me
  And give me signs of future accidents.° *Thunder.*

12 **conjoined** united   20 **repine** complain   5.3.1 **Regent** i.e., York
2 **charming** exercising magic power   2 **periapts** amulets   3 **choice**
excellent   3 **admonish** inform   4 **accidents** events

You speedy helpers, that are substitutes   5
Under the lordly monarch of the north,°
Appear and aid me in this enterprise.

Enter Fiends.

This speedy and quick appearance argues proof
Of your accustomed diligence to me.
Now, ye familiar spirits, that are culled°   10
Out of the powerful regions under earth,
Help me this once, that France may get° the field.
                    They walk, and speak not.
O, hold me not with silence over-long!
Where I was wont to feed you with my blood,
I'll lop a member° off and give it you   15
In earnest° of a further benefit,
So you do condescend to help me now.
                    They hang their heads.
No hope to have redress? My body shall
Pay recompense, if you will grant my suit.
                    They shake their heads.
Cannot my body nor blood-sacrifice   20
Entreat you to your wonted furtherance?°
Then take my soul; my body, soul, and all,
Before that England give the French the f*depart.*
                                    rest
See, they forsake me! Now the *t*
That France must vail° her *'e with.*   25
And let her head fall i*x to the dust.*
My ancient° inca*k fight hand to hand*
And hell too*returns with La Pucelle*
Now, F*r*

the devil (evil spirits were traditionally
regions of the north) 10 **culled** gathered
part of the body 16 **earnest** pledge 21
23 **the foil** defeat, repulse 25 **vail** lower
submission 27 **ancient** former

30   *York.* Damsel of France, I think I have you fast;
         Unchain your spirits now with spelling° charms
         And try if they can gain your liberty.
         A goodly prize, fit for the devil's grace!
         See, how the ugly witch doth bend her brows,
35   As if, with Circe,° she would change my shape!

     Pucelle. Changed to a worser shape thou canst not be.

     York. O, Charles the Dolphin is a proper man;
         No shape but his can please your dainty° eye.

     Pucelle. A plaguing° mischief light on Charles and
         thee!
40   And may ye both be suddenly surprised
         By bloody hands, in sleeping on your beds!

     York. Fell banning° hag, enchantress, hold thy
         tongue!

     Pucelle. I prithee, give me leave to curse awhile.

     York. Curse, miscreant, when thou comest to the
         stake.   *Exeunt.*

     A *rum. Enter Suffolk, with Margaret in his hand.*

45   *Su*   Be what thou wilt, thou art my prisoner.
         O   *Gazes on her.*
         For   auty, do not fear nor fly!
         I kiss   thee but with reverent° hands;
         Who art   for eternal peace
50   *Margaret.* M   on thy tender side.
             king,
             The King of N   may honor thee.
     Suffolk. An earl I a   e, and daughter to a
         Be not offended,

     31 **spelling** spell-casting 35   art.
     the *Odyssey* who transformed
     ous 39 **plaguing** tormenting   lled.
     reverent respectful

Thou art allotted° to be ta'en by me:　　　　　　　　　*55*
So doth the swan her downy cygnets save,
Keeping them prisoner underneath her wings.
Yet if this servile usage° once offend,
Go and be free again as Suffolk's friend.

She is going.

O, stay! [*Aside*] I have no power to let her pass;　　*60*
My hand would free her, but my heart says no.
As plays the sun upon the glassy° streams,
Twinkling another counterfeited° beam,
So seems this gorgeous beauty to mine eyes.
Fain would I woo her, yet I dare not speak;　　　　　*65*
I'll call for pen and ink, and write my mind.
Fie, De la Pole! disable° not thyself.
Hast not a tongue? Is she not here?
Wilt thou be daunted at a woman's sight?
Ay, beauty's princely majesty is such,　　　　　　　*70*
Confounds the tongue and makes the senses
　rough.°

Margaret. Say, Earl of Suffolk, if thy name be so,
　What ransom must I pay before I pass?
　For I perceive I am thy prisoner.

Suffolk. [*Aside*] How canst thou tell she will deny thy
　suit,　　　　　　　　　　　　　　　　　　　*75*
　Before thou make a trial of her love?

Margaret. Why speak'st thou not? What ransom must
　I pay?

Suffolk. [*Aside*] She's beautiful and therefore to be
　wooed;
　She is a woman, therefore to be won.

Margaret. Wilt thou accept of ransom, yea or no?　*80*

Suffolk. [*Aside*] Fond man, remember that thou hast
　a wife;
　Then how can Margaret be thy paramour?

---

55 **allotted** fated　58 **servile usage** unworthy treatment　62 **glassy**
smooth　63 **counterfeited** reflected　67 **disable** disparage　71 **rough**
dull

Margaret. I were best to leave him, for he will not hear.

Suffolk. [*Aside*] There all is marred; there lies a cooling card.°

85 *Margaret.* He talks at random; sure, the man is mad.

Suffolk. [*Still aside, but more loudly*] And yet a dispensation° may be had.

Margaret. And yet I would that you would answer me.

Suffolk. [*Aside*] I'll win this Lady Margaret. For whom?
Why, for my king. [*Somewhat more loudly*] Tush, that's a wooden° thing!

90 *Margaret.* He talks of wood: it° is some carpenter.

Suffolk. [*Aside*] Yet so my fancy may be satisfied
And peace establishèd between these realms.
But there remains a scruple° in that too:
For though her father be the King of Naples,
95 Duke of Anjou and Maine, yet is he poor,
And our nobility will scorn the match.

Margaret. Hear ye, captain, are you not at leisure?

Suffolk. [*Aside*] It shall be so, disdain they ne'er so much:
Henry is youthful and will quickly yield.
100 [*Aloud*] Madam, I have a secret to reveal.

Margaret. [*Aside*] What though I be enthralled?° he seems a knight,
And will not any way dishonor me.

Suffolk. Lady, vouchsafe to listen what I say.

Margaret. [*Aside*] Perhaps I shall be rescued by the French,

---

84 **cooling card** something to cool my ardor   86 **dispensation** i.e., annulment of a previous marriage   89 **wooden** dull   90 **it** he   93 **scruple** difficulty   101 **enthralled** captured

And then I need not crave his courtesy.   *105*

Suffolk. Sweet madam, give me hearing in a cause.

Margaret. [*Aside*] Tush, women have been captivate
   ere now.

Suffolk. Lady, wherefore talk you so?

Margaret. I cry you mercy,° 'tis but *quid* for *quo.*°

Suffolk. Say, gentle princess, would you not suppose   *110*
   Your bondage happy, to be made a queen?

Margaret. To be a queen in bondage is more vile
   Than is a slave in base servility,
   For princes should be free.

Suffolk.   And so shall you,
   If happy England's royal king be free.   *115*

Margaret. Why, what concerns his freedom unto me?

Suffolk. I'll undertake to make thee Henry's queen,
   To put a golden scepter in thy hand
   And set a precious crown upon thy head,
   If thou wilt condescend to be my—

Wh

Sound [a parley]. Enter Reignier on the walls.

See, Reignier, see, thy daughter prisoner!

Reignier. To whom?

Suffolk.   To me.

Reignier.   Suffolk, what remedy?
I am a soldier and unapt° to weep
Or to exclaim on fortune's fickleness.

135 *Suffolk.* Yes, there is remedy enough, my lord:
Consent, and for thy honor give consent,
Thy daughter shall be wedded to my king,
Whom° I with pain° have wooed and won thereto,
And this her easy-held imprisonment
140 Hath gained thy daughter princely liberty.

Reignier. Speaks Suffolk as he thinks?

Suffolk.   Fair Margaret knows
That Suffolk doth not flatter, face,° or feign.

Reignier. Upon thy princely warrant, I descend
___ive thee answer of thy just demand.